CONTENTS

GENERAL EDITOR'S PREFACE

The aim of the Macmillan Master Guides is to help you to appreciate the book you are studying by providing information about it and by suggesting ways of reading and thinking about it which will lead to a fuller understanding. The section on the writer's life and background has been designed to illustrate those aspects of the writer's life which have influenced the work, and to place it in its personal and literary context. The summaries and critical commentary are of special importance in that each brief summary of the action is followed by an examination of the significant critical points. The space which might have been given to repetitive explanatory notes has been devoted to a detailed analysis of the kind of passage which might confront you in an examination. Literary criticism is concerned with both the broader aspects of the work being studied and with its detail. The ideas which meet us in reading a great work of literature, and their relevance to us today, are an essential part of our study, and our Guides look at the thought of their subject in some detail. But just as essential is the craft with which the writer has constructed his work of art, and this may be considered under several technical headings – characterisation, language, style and stagecraft, for example.

The authors of these Guides are all teachers and writers of wide experience, and they have chosen to write about books they admire and know well in the belief that they can communicate their admiration to you. But you yourself must read and know intimately the book you are studying. No one can do that for you. You should see this book as a lamp-post. Use it to shed light, not to lean against. If you know your text and know what it is saying about life, and how it says it, then you will enjoy it, and there is no better way of passing an examination in literature.

JAMES GIBSON

MACMILLAN MASTER GUIDES

SELECTED POEMS

OF T. S. ELIOT

ANDREW SWARBRICK

MACMILLAN
EDUCATION

First edition 1988

Published by
MACMILLAN EDUCATION LTD
Houndmills, Basingstoke, Hampshire RG21 2XS
and London
Companies and representatives throughout the world

Printed in Hong Kong

British Library Cataloguing in Publication Data
Swarbrick, Andrew
Selected poems of T. S. Eliot.—
(Macmillan master guides).
1. Eliot, T. S.—Criticism and
interpretation
I. Title   II. Eliot, T. S.
821'. 912   PS 3509.L43Z/
ISBN 0–333–43702–0 Pbk
ISBN 0–333–43703–9 Pbk export

ACKNOWLEDGEMENTS

The author and publishers wish to thank the following who have kindly given permission for the use of copyright material: Associated Book Publishers (UK) Ltd. for extracts from *The Sacred Wood* by T. S. Eliot, Metheuen and Co; Faber and Faber Ltd. for extracts from *Selected Essays* and *The Use of Poetry and the Use of Criticism* by T. S. Eliot, and *Selected Poems* of T. S. Eliot.

Every effort has been made to trace all the copyright holders but if any have been inadvertently overlooked the publishers will be pleased to make the necessary arrangements at the first opportunity.

Cover illustration: *Thorn Tree* by Graham Sutherland. Photograph © The British Council and reproduced courtesy of the Bridgeman Art Library.

Like every other student since its first appearance, the author is generally indebted to B. C. Southam's *A Student's Guide to the Selected Poems of T. S. Eliot* (Faber & Faber, 1977); specific references are acknowledged in the text.

Author's note: poems which appear under individual headings in *The Complete Poems and Plays of T. S. Eliot* (Faber & Faber, 1969) have their titles italicised in this study; that is, *The Waste Land*, *The Hollow Men*, *Ash-Wednesday* and *Four Quartets*; other titles are rendered in quotation marks.

ANDREW SWARBRICK

For Tom: 30 March 1987

1 T. S. ELIOT:
LIFE AND BACKGROUND

It must often seem to the examination candidate as if Eliot's poetry were deliberately written for the examination-hall. If what it says is difficult enough, the manner of its saying seems even more bewildering: the incomprehensible images, the incoherent syntax, the learned allusions. It must seem an examinee's nightmare, for how can one person, under the duress of an examination, hope to disentangle enough of Eliot's poetry to satisfy the voracious examiner?

It may or may not come as some comfort to know that Eliot himself found his poetry difficult. This was not because he chose to make it so, but because he felt that we live in a difficult age and that in order to comprehend our modern era poetry itself must of necessity be difficult. It may be more comforting to know that your examiner would honestly have to admit to finding Eliot perplexing. Certainly, this writer is aware that even in the brief compass of this study more problems have been raised than solved. The point is this: there is no single 'clue' which will pluck out the heart of Eliot's mystery. It is helpful to know some of the sources of Eliot's allusions and this guide tries to say something about Eliot's use of language in his poems and his major preoccupations; but Eliot's poetry is not a crossword puzzle of clues and solutions. In your thinking and writing about Eliot you should try for honesty. Don't pretend to know what you don't know or to explain what you don't understand. If you can keep your attention on Eliot and not on the examiner, if you say what the poetry makes you feel and not what you think you ought to feel, you might well find, not that the problems disappear, but that they invite you further and further into the poems.

Thomas Stearns Eliot was born in St Louis, Missouri, on 26 September, 1888, the youngest of seven children. His father, Henry Ware Eliot, was a successful businessman and his mother, Charlotte Chauncy Stearns, a woman of exacting taste who took her own writing very seriously. It was altogether a notable family: Eliot's grandfather, William Greenleaf Eliot, was the founder of the first Unitarian church in St Louis and of Washington University. Eliot's family was always aware of its past, and of its Puritan tradition.

In 1909 Eliot graduated from Harvard University where he had developed interests in literature and philosophy; he took his M.A. in 1910 and then went to study in Paris for a year before returning to Harvard to begin his doctoral dissertation on the philosophy of F.H. Bradley. For four years he pursued research and did some teaching, until in 1914 he was awarded a travelling scholarship to Europe. With the outbreak of the First World War, he arrived in Oxford; shortly afterwards he decided to settle in London, to devote himself to poetry and to marry.

His first marriage was to Vivien Haigh-Wood, a woman of artistic inclinations and a nervous disposition. Eliot all too soon found himself burdened by her illnesses and by financial worries: he took up schoolteaching and some part-time lecturing. This left him little time for writing and in 1917 he took up a position with Lloyds Bank in London: his agile mind and linguistic expertise equipped him admirably for his work in the colonial and foreign department. But still it was into the margins of his time that his literary activities were crammed: he wrote numerous reviews and essays and in 1917 *Prufrock and Other Observations* was published. An ever-increasing workload and his wife's ill-health took their toll: in 1921 Eliot was persuaded to take a three-month holiday and to visit Lausanne in Switzerland for psychiatric consultation. It was in Switzerland that he completed *The Waste Land*, at which he had been working since 1919 and which was published in 1922. Eliot returned to London, but not to changed circumstances. Whilst continuing to work at the bank, he founded a new literary journal, *The Criterion*. A group of friends, led by Ezra Pound, had tried to rescue Eliot from the bank by launching a fund for him; the attempt could only have brought embarrassment to a man as independent as Eliot was and, thankfully, nothing came of it. So he remained at Lloyds until 1925, when he became a director of the publishing firm Faber & Gwyer (now Faber & Faber) and embarked on a more congenial career in editing and publishing.

In the mid-1920s Eliot found himself increasingly drawn to Christianity and in 1927 he was confirmed in the Church of England and became a British subject. Both his poetry and criticism reveal Christian sympathies becoming convictions. *The Hollow Men* (1925), 'Journey of the Magi' (1927), *Ash-Wednesday* (1930) and *Four Quartets* (1944) are poems of spiritual quest, while in *The Idea of a Christian Society* (1939) Eliot expressed himself from a fundamental Christian standpoint. In the 1930s Eliot developed his interest in poetic drama: he wrote the choruses for a Christian pageant, *The Rock*, produced in 1934, and in 1935 wrote *Murder in the Cathedral*, a play about the murder of Archbishop Thomas Becket in Canterbury

Cathedral in 1170. Four more plays – *The Family Reunion* (1939), *The Cocktail Party* (1949), *The Confidential Clerk* (1953) and *The Elder Statesman* (1958) – helped to bring Eliot a huge public following which his poetry alone might never have attracted.

In the early 1930s Eliot finally separated from his first wife: he provided for her support but her continuing decline in health and mental stability caused him much anguish and guilt. But by now he was a major public figure in England and America; his wife died in 1947 and the following year he received the Nobel Prize for Literature and the Order of Merit. In 1957 Eliot married Valerie Fletcher who had been his secretary for many years and in these last eight years of his life Eliot found a new personal contentment. He died peacefully on 4 January 1965; his ashes were buried in the village of East Coker from where his ancestors had emigrated to the United States in the seventeenth century and he is memorialised in Westminster Abbey. Amongst the mourners at Eliot's memorial service was the eighty-year-old Ezra Pound. Fifty years earlier he had met Eliot in London and had read over the manuscript of 'The Love Song of J. Alfred Prufrock'; at that moment, a new age in English poetry had been inaugurated.

Despite some notable exceptions, such as Thomas Hardy, English poetry, when Eliot arrived in England in 1914, had all but atrophied. This is not to say that there was no interest in poetry: on the contrary, there existed a sizeable audience for it. But it was an audience which knew what it liked and wanted poetry to flatter its prejudices. It was an audience drawn largely from the upper-middle classes which demanded that poetry confirm its complacent view of itself and of the world. Poetry was to be written in the spirit of public service: to lift the spirits or to console. In his book *The New Poetic*, C. K. Stead offers a close discussion of the poetry written during 1909–16. Here is a representative example, an extract from a poem by Alfred Noyes:

> A voice
> Rough with the storms of many an ocean called,
> 'Drake! Cap'en Drake! The Armada. In the Channel!'
> All eyes were turned on Drake, as he stood there,
> Looming against the sunset and the sea,
> Stiller than bronze. Far off, the first white star
> Gleamed as if motionless in heaven, a world
> Of lonely light and 'wildering speed.
> He tossed
> A grim black ball in the lustrous air and laughed –
> 'Come lads,' he said, 'we've time to finish the game.'
> (quoted in Stead, p.51)

A good question to ask of this sort of thing is: why say it in poetry rather than prose? What has the writer gained in expressiveness by choosing to say what he wants to say in the form of a poem? Nothing more, it seems, than a specious glamour, a conventional respectability with which to treat the well-known story of Drake. The form of poetry is here used as a kind of stage effect, a theatrical device by which to impress the audience with the writer's high-minded seriousness. Poetry is not here explored: is is exploited. On the page it looks like poetry and so summons up in its audience the automatic conviction that what is being said is said beautifully and eloquently, that is, poetically. But simply look at the words. What does a voice 'Rough with the storms of many an ocean' actually sound like? What does the phrase 'as he stood there' tell us, apart from the fact that the poet needed something to fill out the line? Why should Drake be 'looming'? Obviously, Noyes wants to give him heroic proportions, but the language is as vague and imprecise as the emotion Noyes wants to evoke. 'Looming' is surely too sinister, while the phrase 'Stiller than bronze' simply confounds itself: why should bronze be more or less still than anything else? Then we pause for the stage effects about the 'motionless' star, only to be reminded that the star is actually in motion which rather gets in the way of the effects of dramatic stillness and suspense which the poet is trying to produce. But the final flourish gives the game away. We have been told of the sunset and of the first white star: how then can Drake toss his ball in 'the lustrous air'? Such questions are beside the point. The poem moves unthinkingly from one cliché to another, confident that it will find an unthinking and hence approving response to its clichés. This is the poetry of Imperialism, offering the reader an idealised image of England and Englishmen. It is poetry written to please an audience, to tell it what it wants to hear in the guise of bardic inspiration. It is opinion dressed up as poetry.

It is worth labouring the point so that we might appreciate just how shockingly new Eliot must have appeared to his contemporaries. We might realise, too, how stringent and demanding Eliot's first criticial essays were in an intellectual climate which had not only tolerated but praised such writing as we have seen from Noyes, and how urgent was the need to attack the degeneracy of taste. But, by the time Eliot began to make his mark in literary London, the situation was already changing. Even before the outbreak of war in 1914, some of the younger poets were deliberately reacting against the versified Imperialism we have seen above; by the end of the war, nothing was the same.

In 1912 Edward Marsh produced the first of a series of *Georgian Anthologies*. One cannot claim much for most of the poets represented therein except to say that their work represents a marginal but significant change in an attitude to the public: theirs was an attempt

to educate rather than flatter the reader. Some of their poems
address social issues in a politely challenging way and their language
is rather closer to the living language of contemporary speech.
Certainly, they appeared as a sufficient threat to be castigated by
reviewers of an older generation: 'English poetry has been approaching a condition of liberty and licence which threatens, not only to
submerge old standards altogether, but, if persevered in to its logical
limits, to hand over the sensitive art of verse to a general process of
literary democratization.' Elsewhere, Georgian poetry was described
as 'an unrestrained and even violent fashion' (quoted in Stead, p.63).
It is a measure of Eliot's success in establishing new criteria of
judgement that such an opinion can now strike us as being so
comically absurd.

The war of 1914–18 inevitably altered the public perception of
poetry. Of course, poetry was used for propaganda purposes (every
public-spirited poet tried his hand at 'recruiting verses') and cam-
paigns and battles were suitably memorialised in the epic strain. But
as the war went on, the dishonesty of much of this sort of writing
became more painfully glaring. It was as an attempt to report the
truth of war that poets such as Wilfred Owen and Siegfried Sassoon
wrote. Poetry was not for them a cultivated luxury, a leisured
self-indulgence, but a means of prompting action, and some of this
urgency, this revulsion from the horror of life, is to be felt in some of
Eliot's poetry. For Owen, poetry could not be beautiful: 'Above all I
am not concerned with Poetry. My subject is War, and the pity of
War. The Poetry is in the pity'. This is the shock of such pity:

> If in some smothering dreams you too could pace
> Behind the wagon that we flung him in,
> And watch the white eyes writhing in his face,
> His hanging face, like a devil's sick of sin. . . .
>
> ('Dulce et Decorum Est')

In the face of such overwhelming indignation, critics of the old school
began to reverse their earlier opinion that poetry should not be
realistic. As one of the old guard wrote: 'The younger generation,
perceiving that the idyllic school of verse had inevitably exhausted its
capacities, appeared to have set its heart upon proving that no subject
lies intrinsically outside the limits of poetic treatment. . . . The war,
therefore, can be said to have offered our young realists the richest
possible opportunity . . . to speak the truth about the ugly things of
life, and to strip suffering bare of all concealing veils of sentimentality
and pretence. . . . .' (quoted in Stead, p.93). By 1918, it had come to
be realised, the true poets need not be beautiful: but they must be
truthful.

Eliot was not alone in recognising the sterility of English poetry before the war. Another American, Ezra Pound, had, since 1908, been living in London and trying to restore real intelligence and vigour to the world of English letters. A contemporary described him as 'a small but persistent volcano in the dim levels of London literary society' (quoted in Bergonzi, p.28) and by 1914 Pound was beginning to erupt. He was an intensely energetic man with a talent for publicity and for cultivating real poetic ability in others. He had gathered around him a group of poets calling themselves 'Imagists' to which Eliot was loosely attached, and was responsible for the first publication, in 1915, of Eliot's 'The Love Song of J. Alfred Prufrock' in the American magazine *Poetry*. In the following month came Eliot's first publication in England, again under the auspices of Pound, in the Imagist magazine entitled, with suitable aggression, *Blast*. It was Pound who selflessly brought Eliot to the attention of reviewers and editors, who offered Eliot editorial and critical guidance and who was responsible for giving us *The Waste Land* in the form in which we now know it and who is there gratefully acknowledged by Eliot as 'il miglior fabbro' – 'the better craftsman'.

But there were temperamental differences between the two men: Pound was flamboyantly unconventional, enthusiastic and audacious; Eliot was profoundly conventional, moderate and circumspect. It was Pound, eventually to leave England for Italy in disgust at its cultural timidity, who nicknamed Eliot 'Possum' (hence *Old Possum's Book of Practical Cats*) in recognition of Eliot's stealthy assimilation into English manners and, finally, his penetration to the centre of English cultural life. Eliot's achievements in literature are part of a wider movement that earlier this century took place in the arts and which we now call Modernism. But, when Eliot came to prominence in the London of the 1920s, his work was adventurously, even dangerously new, and to miss this historical context is to miss the excitement of his earlier poetry.

2 THEMES

2.1 TRADITION, IMPERSONALITY AND DECADENCE

Eliot's poetry presents us with a most urgent and compelling struggle: the struggle to make language say what we mean it to say. In one of his later poems Eliot described his work as 'a raid on the inarticulate' ('East Coker'): an attempt to say what it is most difficult to say, to express oneself with a completeness of understanding. This, Eliot knew, was the same challenge which had faced every other writer of note before him and as poet and critic he assiduously assimilated himself in the work of his predecessors in order to learn from them. In all of his poetry, Eliot is conscious of precept and example, of undertaking a task that has been undertaken many times before. This is not to say that he modelled himself on previous poets. Far from it. Eliot thought of himself as having been born into an age of crisis, of the disintegration of old beliefs and old ways of life. His was a task not of perpetuating a tradition, but of recovering something lost. He did not simply imitate his masters, for he had to find new ways of saying new things. He had to be revolutionary, but only in order to effect a restoration. So at the heart of Eliot's poetry is a contemplation of the past and of the idea of tradition.

In an essay published in 1919 – 'Tradition and the Individual Talent' – Eliot considers the proper relationship between the contemporary writer and the past. Its central thesis is that literary tradition is not to be considered as something belonging to the past, dead and buried, but as a living presence with the writer. The great works of the past are to be perceived not as relics, but as having a contemporaneous existence with the writer. These works compose an order to which the new writer contributes, and in contributing to that order he also modifies its internal relations. Thus 'tradition' takes on a living force of its own. It is the writer's life-blood and the writer is both partaking of and contributing to that tradition in every work of art he produces. It follows for Eliot, then, that in his art the writer is expressing not himself, not his individually unique personality, but something of the tradition itself.

In his essay Eliot defines his understanding of tradition as a historical sense which perceives not only the pastness of the past, but also its presence. It 'compels a man to write not merely with his own generation in his bones, but with a feeling that the whole of the literature of Europe from Homer and within it the whole of the literature of his own country has a simultaneous existence and composes a simultaneous order' (*Selected Essays*, p.14). The new poet is significant only in his relation to past poets and in his writing he must be conscious that the new work of art he produces will alter, however slightly, the current of tradition. Hence, the past may be altered by the present 'as much as the present is directed by the past' (p.15). In order to recognise and assimilate himself within the literary tradition, the poet must avoid mere self-expression. Instead, he must observe himself almost as a scientist observes a chemical reaction. The poet is a medium 'in which special, or very varied, feelings are at liberty to enter into new combinations' (p.18) and in this way what the poet writes is not self-expression, but something more impersonal which seeks to express the tradition which has shaped his language and to which he now gives a new shape. 'What happens is a continual surrender of himself as he is at the moment to something which is more valuable. The progress of an artist is a continual self-sacrifice, a continual extinction of personality' (p.17).

Much of this thinking shows itself in the technical aspects of Eliot's poetry: his use of personae, or masks, such as the character of Prufrock or Gerontion to achieve an impersonality, or the use of allusions to synthesise past and present. Some of these aspects are dealt with elsewhere in this study. The thematic importance of Eliot's almost reverential perception of the English and European literary tradition lies in the attitude his poetry takes to modern civilisation. Everywhere in Eliot's poems is a sense of disgust for modern life, a conviction that civilised values have been betrayed. Eliot elevates the idea of tradition to such a commanding status because contemporary life seemed to offer him no other object of veneration. This seems true at least until the time Eliot began to look towards Christianity as a source of order and value: one might almost say that the perception of tradition was for Eliot a precursor to the perception of God.

Eliot's early poetry is frequently taken up with cosmopolitan life. 'The Love Song of J. Alfred Prufrock', 'Portrait of a Lady', 'Preludes' and 'Rhapsody on a Windy Night' each take place in a setting of urban society. Prufrock is terrorised by women's eyes which seem to pin him against the wall, obsessed by what they will say of his receding hair, his thinness. Society as portrayed in 'Portrait of a Lady' is 'cultured' only in the most pretentious and artificial way, the Lady's neurosis representative of a society living on its nerves. The city portrayed in the 'Preludes' is essentially the same city as that described by Prufrock with its 'one-night cheap hotels/And sawdust restaurants': the 'Preludes' gives us the 'newspapers from vacant lots' blowing in the wind, the 'sawdust-trampled street', 'a blackened street' and 'ancient women/Gathering fuel in vacant lots'. The quality of life in such a setting is meagre, empty of everything except routine, offering only fear and loneliness for the girl who at night watches 'The thousand sordid images/Of which your soul was constituted'. This is a world of deadening monotony, of crushing purposelessness. It is a world of unthinking self-gratification, of lovelessness. The woman glimpsed in 'Rhapsody on a Windy Night' is probably a prostitute and the action of 'Sweeney Erect' takes place in a brothel. Sweeney is modern man, 'Broadbottomed', rising with 'Gesture of orang-outang'; modern woman is the girl in the 'Preludes' grasping 'the yellow soles of feet/In the palms of both soiled hands', or the epileptic 'clutching at her sides' in 'Sweeney Erect', or the uncomprehending Doris who 'towelled from the bath,/Enters padding on broad feet'.

And so the speaker of the 'Preludes' and 'Rhapsody on a Windy Night' tramps the streets, aimless, lonely and fearful. Life seems random, chaotic, meaningless, the modern city a nightmarish symbol of humanity's inveterate decadence.

2.2   DEATH-IN-LIFE AND LIFE-IN-DEATH

In fact, life as perceived in the early poems is barely worth the name. It is not life, but existence: valueless and without purpose. Modern life in Eliot's poetry quickly becomes a living Hell, as suggested by the epigraph to 'The Love Song' or the portrayal of London in the first poem of *The Waste Land* entitled 'The Burial of the Dead'. At its most nightmarish, that is what modern life became to Eliot, oppressed as he was at that time by exhaustion, mental illness and personal unhappiness. The city is a burial-chamber in which ghosts wander: 'Sighs, short and infrequent, were exhaled,/And each man fixed his eyes before his feet' (*The Waste Land*). This is not life, but death-in-life, a living death.

Gerontion is a figure of death-in-life. He is 'an old man in a dry month . . . waiting for rain'. He is 'A dull head among windy spaces', 'An old man in a draughty house/Under a windy knob' where 'Vacant shuttles/Weave the wind'. In his 'sleepy corner', he struggles to utter his 'Thoughts of a dry brain in a dry season'. The symbolism bears close affinities to that of *The Waste Land* (to which Eliot intended to attach 'Gerontion' as a prelude) with its stone, rubble, and deserts, its awaiting of rain. In *The Hollow Men* we are given figures stuffed with straw, their 'dried voices . . . quiet and meaningless', gathered on the beach of a river (and awaiting its crossing, perhaps like the souls of the damned who cross the river Styx in Hades). The poem speculates about 'death's other Kingdom' and 'death's dream kingdom' in a way that suggests current life is not the opposite of death but only another territory in the kingdom of Death.

Other of Eliot's poems similarly portray twentieth-century man as condemned to a living death. At the heart of his damned condition lies an inability to love and a confusion between love and the carnal gratifications of sex. Prufrock cannot write his love song and feels threatened by women, 'The eyes that fix you in a formulated phrase'; there is also a shiver of revulsion at the sight of 'Arms that are braceleted and white and bare/(But in the lamplight, downed with light brown hair!)'. The vision of womanhood at the poem's conclusion remains mystical and idealised: 'sea-girls wreathed with seaweed red and brown'. The girl in the 'Preludes' has a soul constituted by a 'thousand sordid images' and in the morning is to be found taking the curlers from her hair. The epileptic girl in 'Sweeney Erect' is described in grossly physical terms, her mouth 'This oval O cropped out with teeth' and her epileptic fit is portrayed in a manner ambiguously suggestive of the sexual act. Elsewhere women are to be identified as prostitutes, or else as the almost sub-human Doris, 'padding on broad feet'. Eliot's poems show a Puritan rectitude in the face of sexuality. In 'Whispers of Immortality', the figure of Grishkin has a feline seductiveness: 'Uncorseted, her friendly bust/Gives promise of pneumatic bliss', but we feel the scornful contempt in the witty conjunction of 'bliss' with the mechanical word 'pneumatic'. And in the eyes of Eliot's personae, sexual relations have indeed become mechanical. Occasionally, there is a surge of real longing: Prufrock's vision of the mermaids or the hyacinth girl in *The Waste Land* or in *Ash-Wednesday* the 'broadbacked figure drest in blue and green' who suddenly prompts the delight of 'Blown hair is sweet, brown hair over the mouth blown,/Lilac and brown hair'.

But it is the speaker of 'Portrait of a Lady' who represents the more characteristic attitude. He stubbornly resists the emotional demands made of him by the Lady. He is trapped in a society of artifice, with its mannered proprieties and brittle ennui. He feels himself a performer on the social stage: he must 'dance, dance/Like a dancing bear,/Cry like a parrot, chatter like an ape'. Lacking the courage to express his true feelings to the Lady (and perhaps he does not truly know what they are), the speaker is caught in a tortuous compromise, visiting the woman but remaining passively unresponsive to her. He is governed by a self-protective impulse. He keeps his countenance, he remains self-possessed: he fears a closer contact with humanity. His relations with the Lady are tepid, born out of habit rather than feeling. And this seems to be generally true of the human relationships in Eliot's poems: one sort of character (Prufrock, the speaker of 'Portrait of a Lady') timidly withdraws from relationships; another sort (Sweeney, 'the young man carbuncular' in *The Waste Land*) is incapable of forming a relationship because of the selfish obsession with the mere gratification of physical appetite. In this sort of attitude Eliot fearfully perceives a vulgarity which cripples any capacity for spiritual growth.

In coming to understand life as a living death, Eliot also came to understand that to embark on a new life required a kind of death, a complete and uncaring renunciation of an old way of life. *The Hollow Men* is a poem which seems to be approaching this sort of perception. There is a yearning for the place of 'Sunlight' and singing voices, but also a fear of it, an instinct to evade it by 'deliberate disguises'. In the fragmented ending of the poem, the beginning of a prayer is blurted out, but intervening is 'the Shadow', the shadow of the Holy Spirit, perhaps, which prompts longing and fear, hope and despair. These feelings are made more explicit in 'Journey of the Magi'. Witnessing the Nativity was an occasion not of blessedness, but of perplexity:

> . . . were we led all that way for
> Birth or Death? There was a Birth, certainly,
> We had evidence and no doubt. I had seen birth and death,
> But had thought they were different; this Birth was
> Hard and bitter agony for us, like Death, our death.

The magus does not doubt that he saw a birth, but knows that this Birth also entails a Death, the death of an old way of life in which he is 'no longer at ease'. The poem was written at a time when Eliot was preparing himself for confirmation in the Church of England and he was received into the Church in 1927. In December of that year, Section II of *Ash-Wednesday* appeared under the title 'Salutation' and Section I was published a few months later. Like 'Journey of the Magi', these poems express the advent of Christian acceptance as requiring a painful as well as joyful readjustment of attitudes. In Section II of *Ash-Wednesday*, a body has been dismembered in order to achieve a kind of purification. The first Section opens with a reference to conversion – a turning: 'Because I do not hope to turn again . . . ' and asserts that, in order not to turn again, the speaker must accept that thus far his life has amounted to nothing – more, he must rejoice that he has now 'to construct something/Upon which to rejoice'. So, in order to reconstruct himself into a new life, there must be a preliminary destruction: Birth is accompanied by Death. The corollary of death-in-life is that there be life-in-death.

2.3 IN SEARCH OF THE DIVINE: LOVE AND TIME

Eliot's conversion to Christianity in 1927 came as something of a surprise to his friends. The poet who had so clearly described in his poems the anguish of contemporary civilisation, and in doing so had seemed to speak for his generation, appeared to have performed a volte-face in asserting his Christian beliefs. With the luxury of hindsight, we might now see that from the first Eliot's poems were a personal exploration of his spiritual condition and that always present in them is a longing for redemption. Prufrock has his vision of mermaids, Gerontion of rain, the Hollow Men of the 'perpetual star' and 'Multifoliate rose'. Having been made the representative voice of a sceptical, atheistic and scientific age, Eliot disclaimed that his earlier poetry asserted the impossibility of belief. His sense of desolation, he said, did not deny the presence of belief: on the contrary, he wrote, 'doubt and uncertainty are merely a variety of belief'. In other words, Eliot's Christian beliefs were arrived at only after a long period of struggle, and indeed his Christianity was always a difficult possession, always requiring a spiritual strenuousness. Eliot well knew of 'the demon of doubt which is inseparable from the spirit of belief' (*Selected Essays*, p.411).

Ash-Wednesday is perhaps the poem which most fully expresses these aspects of Eliot's spiritual journey. It presents us with particular difficulties in that so much of its symbolism is drawn from the Italian poet Dante (1265–1321) who in his *Divine Comedy* expressed with a glorious visual fullness the spiritual journey from Hell to Paradise. Eliot had immersed himself in the reading of Dante for many years and it seems natural that at the time of his conversion he felt a particular kinship with him. But Eliot never gives utterance to his Christian beliefs without also expressing the personal struggles they have entailed. The pain of renunciation is present in Section I behind the conviction that from renunciation there will grow a new life; in Section II, the attitude of Christian humility is conceived of as a dismemberment and emptying of the self. The third Section is unambiguous in its affirmation of an erotic attraction which is denied only with great difficulty. On the staircase of spiritual ascent, the penitent is assailed by the 'Distraction' of a female figure of enchanting loveliness and he must call upon a 'strength beyond hope and despair' to overcome worldly desire. The fifth poem presents the penitent as 'torn', and appealing for divine intercession: 'Will the veiled sister pray/For children at the gate/Who will not go away and cannot pray . . . '. *Ash-Wednesday* is not a statement of belief. Eliot's Christianity was never so secure as a list of dogma to which he passively subscribed. Rather, these poems express the impulse to believe, the desire for a supernatural order, a craving as often thwarted as satisfied.

Throughout his life Eliot had a passion for order. His manners were impeccable, his bearing fastidious. To a man such as Eliot who valued self-control, discretion and restraint ('Poetry is not a turning loose of emotion, but an escape from emotion,' he wrote in 'Tradition and the Individual Talent'), the unhappiness of his first marriage was a personal nightmare. One cannot but feel that in part the consolations of Christianity offered at this time a source of comfort and solace, however rare such moments may actually have been. Moreover Eliot found in the structure of Christian belief an ordered system which satisfied his own temperamental inclinations towards rationality and harmony. It came to seem to Eliot that Christianity offered a comprehensible account of the mortal world as he had come to perceive it:

> He finds the world to be so and so; he finds its character inexplicable by any non-religious theory: among religions he finds Christianity, and Catholic Christianity, to account most satisfactorily for the world and especially for the moral world within; and thus . . . he finds himself inexorably committed to the dogma of the Incarnation (*Selected Essays*, p.408)

'The moral world within. . . .'. This is the experience for which Eliot sought expression and validity in the tenets of Christian faith. The feelings of disgust which overwhelm the early poetry are the negative side of an impulse towards the pursuit of beauty. The ultimate beauty to which Eliot was drawn, and which is most lovingly expressed in parts of *Ash-Wednesday* and 'Burnt Norton', is the beauty of divine love. For Eliot the experience of human love only makes sense as a mortal version of an ultimately divine love:

> Grace to the Mother
> For the Garden
> Where all love ends.
>
> (*Ash-Wednesday*)

According to Christian theology, the moment when divine love intervened most clearly in mortal existence was the moment of the Incarnation when, through the Virgin Mary, God took on the flesh of humanity in order to be manifest in the presence of Jesus Christ to share in mankind's suffering, and in the Resurrection to assert the promise of eternity. It is tempting to see the idea of the Incarnation appearing in Eliot's poetry even as early as the 'Preludes':

> I am moved by fancies that are curled
> Around these images, and cling:
> The notion of some infinitely gentle
> Infinitely suffering thing.

The Incarnation came to represent for Eliot an historical moment when the ultimate truth of divine love made itself manifest and so gave point and purpose to human relationships: 'the love of man and woman . . . is only explained and made reasonable by the higher love, or else is simply the coupling of animals' (*Selected Essays*, p.274). The early poems show human 'love' as no more than animal coupling and this explains the revulsion from human closeness to be found in them; the later poems show human love as transfigured by its origin in divine love, 'Where all love ends'.

As well as representing the moment when God's love showed itself to man, the Incarnation is also theologically significant in manifesting an intersection of historical time and eternity. Historical time is time as mortality knows it, the passage of one year to another, one day to another, one moment to another. It is linear, a sequence of passing moments, a temporal successiveness. Eternity is time*less*, the absence of time, a perpetual stillness. Eliot's conversion to Christianity brought with it a new attitude to time which we can see developing in his poems.

In the early poems, time is a heavy burden to be endured. Prufrock is appalled when he looks into the future, for all he sees is a grinding repetition of tedium, habit, boredom:

> There will be time, there will be time
> To prepare a face to meet the faces that you meet;
> There will be time to murder and create,
> And time for all the works and days of hands . . .

Time is an inexorable process of decay – 'I grow old . . . I grow old . . . ' – and a medium of constant change and alteration: 'In a minute there is time/For decisions and revisions which a minute will reverse'. In the 'Preludes' and 'Rhapsody on a Windy Night', the onward flow of time is felt in the leaden beats of the rhythm as well as in the repetitive sequence of hours and days that the poems describe. In 'The Love Song of J. Alfred Prufrock', the very technique of the poem is an effort to escape the onward successiveness of time. The narrative structure of the poem is fugitive: it is hard to locate an ordering of past, present and future or of beginning, middle and end. The temporal relations between the parts of the poem – what events happened in what order – are deliberately blurred. The poem's fragmentariness, the jumbling of time-scales, is an attempt to escape the narrative sequence of past-present-future to create a simultaneity, a synchrony which suggests that what happens in the poem happens all at once – memory and expectation, action and reflection. The effect is to displace normal temporal relations rather as a Cubist painting dislodges normal spatial relations.

In trying to make sense of life, Eliot had to make sense of time, to find some value and purpose in the otherwise meaningless transitoriness of birth, decay and death. Gerontion is an old man who has lost his active faculties, who now looks back over his life and sees not pattern but chaos. Time, or 'History', has deceived him, led him down corridors, appealed to his vanities. In wondering whether the spider will 'Suspend its operations' or the 'weevil/Delay', Gerontion seems also to be wondering whether time will finally stand still and reveal the purpose to which it has been intending. In *The Hollow Men* the final section seems to hint at the senseless repetitiousness of time in the menacing fragment of a nursery rhyme. But in *Ash-Wednesday* mortal time is seen to have meaning and purpose. In Section IV, which seems to be an address to a figure resembling the Virgin Mary, the speaker asks that she 'Redeem/The time'. Human history is redeemed, granted salvation, by the moment when God used the Virgin Mary as the instrument of the Incarnation, when eternity participated in mortality to show that there is a purpose in human history: a knowledge of God. In his choruses written to accompany a verse pageant-play called *The Rock* in 1934, Eliot wrote:

Then came, at a predetermined moment, a moment in time and of
    time,
A moment not out of time, but in time, in what we call history:
    transecting, bisecting the world of time, a moment in time but
    not like a moment of time,
A moment in time but time was made through that moment: for
    without the meaning there is no time, and that moment of time
    gave the meaning.

(Section VII)

If we forgive Eliot his gnostic style (imitative of Biblical utterance and the choric style of Greek tragedy), we should understand that the moment here honoured is the moment when God took on human form in the Incarnation and thus redeemed time by revealing eternity.

At this point, we might need to remind ourselves that in his later poems Eliot was not writing religious propaganda or a poetry of religious statement. Eliot's poems are not sermons or persuasions towards Christian belief. The non-Christian reader is not placed thereby at a disadvantage in reading these poems. Whilst the poems might deal with highly complex concepts, they remain, above all, *poetry*, although the Christian believer is likely to respond to them with a more passionate assent. The concepts of time in 'Burnt Norton' are indeed puzzling, but the poetry shows itself in the masterly control of statement and image, of rhythm, cadence and feeling. For instance, in Section IV the poem shrinks to the single word 'Chill', almost as in a shiver, before moving expansively outwards to the vision of the kingfisher's wing catching the sunlight – a movement towards warmth, fullness and illumination. As well as seeking timeless moments, the poem also explores the activity of poetry itself as an effort to achieve stillness, 'as a Chinese jar still/Moves perpetually in its stillness'. In the framework of belief in which the poem lodges itself, 'Burnt Norton' is undoubtedly Christian: but it is also an affirmation of faith in the meaningfulness of life.

3 THE POEMS

3.1 'THE LOVE SONG OF J. ALFRED PRUFROCK'

'The Love Song of J. Alfred Prufrock' is neither a song nor a conventional expression of love. The identity of 'J. Alfred Prufrock' – a comically ridiculous name for a love-poet – remains blurred, while the other figures referred to in the poem are fleeting and insubstantial. The poem thrives on indefiniteness. Its title promises a love song but what it actually delivers is a fragmentary collage of false starts, hesitations and digressions. For J. Alfred Prufrock, a love song proves impossible. His poem is thus an ironic attack against the easy sentimentalities and clichés popularly associated with the love song. In Prufrock's (and Eliot's) hands, it falls apart into fragments, collapses into inarticulateness. It is worth remembering from the outset that the strategy of the poem is comic, although a dreadful seriousness underlies the comedy.

Why is Prufrock incapable of a love song? Partly, this is due to Prufrock's own personality but the reason also has to do with the difficulties with which language presents us. Prufrock's problem is that he is paralysed by an acute self-consciousness. Like Prince Hamlet, whom he claims not to resemble, Prufrock is unable to act decisively. Forever brooding and speculating on action, he is in reality inadequate to action and to the emotional commitment implied by a love song. His poem begins conventionally enough:

> Let us go then, you and I,
> When the evening is spread out against the sky . . .

This has an appropriately lyrical note (notice the rhyming couplet), a romantic setting and appears to be initiating a situation full of possibilities. The 'you', we immediately assume, is Prufrock's lover (though we shall never actually have it identified). Then the lyricism suddenly collapses. Trying to find a simile to describe the evening,

Prufrock comes up with 'Like a patient etherised upon a table'. We could spend a lot of time – many critics have – trying to decide in what ways an evening is like an etherised patient. The point is, surely, that the image is comically inappropriate. Already, by the third line of the poem, Prufrock's love song has faltered. He tries again. 'Let us go, through certain half-deserted streets. . . .' For seven lines we progress through these streets, their cheap hotels and restaurants suggesting urban decay. A sequence of rhyming couplets is achieved (notice that the line about the etherised patient remains unrhymed) and a metaphor is established by which the winding streets, crossing and re-crossing themselves, are identified with a tortuous train of thought, a 'tedious argument/Of insidious intent/To lead you to an overwhelming question . . . '. This, we feel, is getting us somewhere: as he walks these streets with the 'you' of the first line, Prufrock is preoccupied with a familiar line of thought ('a tedious argument') the movement of which, in his mind, becomes identified with the streets themselves. A resolution is reached which will lead to 'an overwhelming question'. But the question is never asked. The dramatic pause, signified by the dots, is deflated by 'Oh, do not ask, "What is it?"/Let us go and make our visit'. The bathos is felt in the doggerel rhyme and rhythm of the couplet. The question is left hanging in the air; it is a question which Prufrock comically fails to ask in the rest of the poem.

'The room' of women is, we may suppose, the object of this 'visit'. The women talk of 'Michelangelo' and we imagine the cultivated tones of civilised conversation, sophisticated, refined and utterly hollow, like the silly rhyme between 'go' and the mellifluous 'Michelangelo'. Then there follows a passage about the fog which 'rubs', 'Licked', 'Lingered' and finally 'curled once about the house, and fell asleep'. The metaphorical associations between the fog and a cat are clear enough (this is, remember, from the author of *Old Possum's Book of Practical Cats*). But what, we may ask, is this extended metaphor doing in this poem – a 'Love Song' – at this point? The passage represents Prufrock's imaginative flight of fancy. It comes after the couplet mocking the women in the room. Quite simply, it shows us that Prufrock wishes he were somewhere else than with these chattering women and their arty conversation. His mind wanders and lingers with what is outside rather than inside the room. There is something very comforting about the sinuous, silky, cat-like movements of the fog. They represent an ease and contentment which Prufrock, with these women, is very far from feeling. The intensifying association of the fog with a cat is an imaginative *jeu d'esprit*, a triumphant little game as Prufrock finds the words to make the fog like a cat. The final two lines, more rhythmically certain than the others and with an emphatic concluding rhyme, have the naive, inventive pleasure of a children's story. The passage is escapist, a distraction – for the reader as for Prufrock – from the room in which Prufrock is unwillingly trapped.

In this drawing-room setting of brittle politeness and conversation, Prufrock is both agitated and bored, a sensation which Eliot captures in his long sentences and obsessive repetitions. Prufrock knows this milieu all too well. He sees time stretching before him, unalterably repeating situations like this one, constantly demanding decisions, answers to questions, presenting him with choices to be made, 'To wonder, "Do I dare?" and "Do I dare?"'. He must always put on the performance of social ease, 'To prepare a face to meet the faces that you meet'. Decisiveness is illusory, for he will always have the choice to reverse and revise his decisions. Hence, all choices, whether great or small, are reduced to meaninglessness. The onward process of time renders our choices ineffectual for we can never foresee their consequences. Thus, 'Do I dare/Disturb the universe?' is, as the dramatic enjambment hints, self-mocking; Prufrock knows that 'In a minute there is time/For decisions and revisions which a minute will reverse'. He is powerless and feels threatened by 'The eyes that fix you in a formulated phrase'. He is self-consciously aware of himself as a performer, aware of how he appears to other people, '(They will say: "How his hair is growing thin!")', conscious of being scrutinised by them. His life seems only an accumulation of such worthless moments – 'I have measured out my life with coffee spoons' – amounting to nothing more than tedious routine:

> Then how should I begin
> To spit out all the butt-ends of my days and ways?

So his own existence is contemptuously dismissed, an existence characterised by boredom and fear, the fear of acting decisively and the boredom of social existence. The passage about the women's arms reveals the same sort of fastidiousness before life. Although he is responsive to the women's 'Arms that are braceleted and white and bare', we feel Prufrock's shudder of distaste when he notices that they are 'downed with light brown hair!'. This is hardly the sensibility of a man writing a love song. As he says, 'And should I then presume?/And how should I begin?' Once more he makes an attempt, before his three lines about the men leaning out of windows drift into silence. The effort ends with another image of escape: 'I should have been a pair of ragged claws/Scuttling across the floors of silent seas'. The passage about the fog showed us Prufrock wanting to escape the room of women. Now his yearning is for complete isolation, for the unbroken darkness and silence of the sea's floor, for the inconsequential scuttling of the crab.

But Prufrock remains tormented by the choice of whether or not to bring some matter to a head: 'Should I, after tea and cakes and ices,/Have the strength to force the moment to its crisis?'. It seems not: he is 'no prophet – and here's no great matter'. His sense of futility overwhelms him. He may suffer ('though I have wept and fasted'), he may be punished, but even here he cannot resist self-mockery in deliberately sounding Biblical echoes and throwing in the bathetic joke about his head, on a platter, having grown slightly bald. He sees himself as an object of derision, being snickered at even by the 'eternal Footman' who holds his coat. But finally a more sombre note emerges from the self-mockery: 'And in short, I was afraid'.

anti-climax

Now, retrospectively, Prufrock wonders whether it would 'have been worth it, after all, . . . To have bitten off the matter with a smile' if, he having asked his 'overwhelming question', the woman should say ' "That is not what I meant at all./That is not it, at all" '. Angrily, perhaps guiltily, he rejects a leading role for himself. He is not Prince Hamlet but a minor player in the drama, 'a bit obtuse;/At times, indeed, almost ridiculous – /Almost, at times, the Fool'. And then, like the Fool who conventionally utters wisdom under the guise of idiocy, Prufrock once more mocks himself. The gravity of 'I grow old . . . I grow old . . . ' is punctured by the absurd shift of tone to 'I shall wear the bottoms of my trousers rolled'. He mocks his own indecision, wondering whether to adopt the latest fashion and part his hair behind or whether to eat a peach. He imagines himself as an old man walking on the beach. But suddenly, mention of the beach recalls the 'mermaids' he has heard singing there and with this comes a beatific vision of loveliness, release, fulfilment:

> I have seen them riding seaward on the waves
> Combing the white hair of the waves blown back
> When the wind blows the water white and black.

It is this interior vision that Prufrock wants to enter into and preserve. But he knows that he is excluded: 'I do not think that they will sing to me'. He is excluded because he is human, constantly pulled back to the realm of humanity, to Prince Hamlet's 'sterile promontory'. He is 'drowned' not when he lingers with the sea-girls 'in the chambers of the sea' but when 'human voices wake us'.

What then do we know of Prufrock's personality? The poem expresses a state of indecision, incapacity, self-contempt and a despair relieved only by a recollected vision of other-worldly beauty. The poem purports to be a love song, but fails. We never know what Prufrock's 'overwhelming question' is and he never manages to ask it. But since he is trying to write a love song, we may suppose that the question has to do with his relationship with a woman, the 'you' of the first line and the 'one' who settles a pillow by her head and who, he imagines, would have reacted to his question with incomprehension. The setting of the poem places Prufrock in a group of women who seem to threaten him: he is 'sprawling on a pin . . . wriggling on the wall' and he is both fascinated and revolted by the hair on their arms. He is intimidated by these women and overwhelmed by a sense of futility. His unasked question may be to invite a declaration of love or a proposal of marriage. But, given Prufrock's self-paralysing indecisiveness, his timorousness, the question may be an utterly insignificant one which, in his state of almost comical bewilderment, has reached overwhelming proportions. A man who, at a party, wonders 'Do I dare to eat a peach?' is likely to be one who cannot bring himself to ask a meaningful question.

But although Prufrock is not the man for a love song, he does have a notion of love. The closing vision of the mermaids is an image of feminine purity and beauty which represents idealised womanhood. For Prufrock, women in reality fall short of this ideal. Prufrock has to preserve his vision by retreating from the real world; his idealised notion of love is in danger of being contaminated by his real experience of women. To escape the real world, to attain the condition of the crab 'Scuttling across the floors of silent seas' seems to be the effort of Prufrock's love song. But the failure of Prufrock's love song is the result not only of his personality, nor only of the disparity between the ideal and the actual, but also of the failure to find a language by which to express himself fully.

Towards the end of the poem, Prufrock bursts out with 'It is impossible to say just what I mean!' Similarly, the unidentified woman is imagined as saying ' "That is not what I meant at all" '. The poem is preoccupied with its own thwarted attempts to say anything. Almost as a refrain, the poem questions how it should proceed: 'So how should I presume? . . . Then how should I begin/To spit out all the butt-ends of my days and ways? . . . And how should I begin? . . . Shall I say . . . ?' The fragments that make up the poem are a collection of possible poems all of which collapse because the speaker cannot find the language for his 'overwhelming question' and cannot know what the question is until he has found the language for it.

Language continually fails him. The first paragraph never arrives at the question; instead, it escapes into a jokily bathetic couplet: 'Oh, do not ask, "What is it?"/Let us go and make our visit'. Then we have a little poem about the fog which slips from the present tense to the past as if conscious of itself as something complete, a little unit resting amongst other units. One of the units begins 'Shall I say, I have gone at dusk through narrow streets . . . ?' only to end two lines later with an image of its speaker as 'a pair of ragged claws/Scuttling across the floors of silent seas'. Here, perhaps, we see the image of the writer as a pair of claws, thumb and forefinger, scuttling sideways with a pen across the paper and failing to break the silence of the sea-floors. Prufrock's effort in the poem is to wrestle with his own inarticulateness, the obduracy of language which resists his attempts to make it mean what he wants it to mean. This may sound philosophically remote, but only consider your own difficulties in expressing yourself – how a page of writing is covered in crossings-out and alterations. Like Prufrock, like Eliot, you too know the resistance of language.

Let us return to the beginning. The poem's epigraph comes from the *Inferno* of the medieval Italian poet Dante. Its speaker is in Hell, speaking to Dante through the quivering tip of a flame. He speaks only because he assumes that Dante, like him, will not be able to return from Hell. 'If I thought that my reply would be to someone who would ever return to earth, this flame would remain without further movement; but as no one has ever returned alive from this gulf, if what I hear is true, I can answer you with no fear of infamy' (Eliot's translation). Prufrock too is speaking in a sort of Hell and, as with Dante's speaker, his utterance is achieved only through great difficulty. Prufrock's state of anguish is largely brought about because he is condemned to use a language by which he cannot perfectly express himself. He is excluded from the mermaids' song. He is suffocated and drowned by his human voice.

The 'meaning' of the poem, then, emerges from its form: the digressions, intrusions and hesitations themselves express Prufrock's incapacity. The poem does possess a unifying principle for its cohesiveness lies within the consciousness of its speaker. The seemingly random perceptions, statements and questions are fused in the mind of Prufrock. The exterior world of fog, rooms and women is mingled with the interior world of the mind that perceives it. This interior world is a continuous flux of feelings, thoughts, doubts, speculations, self-questionings. The poem presents us not just with the thoughts and feelings of Prufrock, but with the very experience of his thinking and feeling. Eliot is not primarily interested in creating a fully-rounded personality, a dramatic character called Prufrock, but in rendering the activity of the mind. Things happen to and in that mind and what we hear is its interior voice trying to tell us of itself, to express its activity. Although we might say something about the 'personality' of Prufrock and the situation 'he' is in, it is the movement of his mind and its self-awareness which constitute the substance of the poem.

3.2 'PORTRAIT OF A LADY'

Like 'The Love Song of J. Alfred Prufrock', 'Portrait of a Lady' is written in the first person and deals with the speaker's relationship with a woman. The 'Lady' of the title has been identified as Adeleine

Moffat, an elderly Boston socialite whom Eliot used to visit and the social milieu of the poem once again suggests the drawing-room world of cosmopolitan fashion and sophistication. The title refers directly to a novel by the American writer Henry James (1843–1916) who, like Eliot, exiled himself for most of his life in England and immersed himself in European culture. James's *Portrait of a Lady* (published in 1881) is a minutely observed psychological exploration of an American woman in Europe and her various relationships which culminate in a ruinous marriage. Eliot's poem catches the psychological intensity of James's writing, the tone of aloof detachment and the punctiliousness of phrasing and vocabulary (for example, 'velleities', 'attenuated tones of violins').

The three sections of the poem describe three visits – in December, April and October – made by the speaker to the Lady. On each occasion the Lady seems to want to develop with the speaker an intimacy which he resists. The emotions which the speaker's reluctance with the Lady causes him to feel – complacency, guilt, hostility, self-disgust – are caught in the poem not as definite states of feeling definitely described, but as a nexus or vortex of inseparable feelings which are forever shifting and merging. The poem is the speaker's attempt to articulate his emotions, to try to identify and account for his emotional state, to find the *mot juste* by which to render his feelings intelligible to himself. As in 'The Love Song of J. Alfred Prufrock', we find an indissoluble union of thought and feeling as the poet's intellect is turned in on his own emotions. This blend of thought and feeling is what Eliot so admired in the poetry of the Metaphysical poets such as John Donne (1571?–1631) who were able to 'feel their thought as immediately as the odour of a rose' (*Selected Essays*, p.287).

The first section portrays a visit to the Lady in December. Immediately, we are in an atmosphere of artificiality. The 'scene' is arranged so as to appear unpremeditated, as if the Lady wants to pass off as natural a setting which she has arranged with the meticulous care of a set-designer. Hence, the reference to 'Juliet's tomb' (from Shakespeare's *Romeo and Juliet*) is a telling one: this Lady's room is *stagey*, elaborately calculated to induce a particular mood. There is something romantically decadent about the room with its four wax candles producing 'Four rings of light upon the ceiling overhead' (Juliet's tomb, we remember, is the *locus classicus* of thwarted passion and tragic irony). This darkened room is the stage, 'Prepared for all the things to be said, or left unsaid', on which the speaker will have to perform before the Lady, though this line makes it clear that the speaker is not entirely sure of the script he should follow.

This visit seems to have followed a concert performance from 'the latest Pole' playing Chopin's 'Preludes'. Now we hear a snatch of conversation about Chopin. What do you think is our attitude to the speaker of the lines about Chopin? Look at the vocabulary: 'intimate . . . soul . . . resurrected . . . touch the bloom . . . '. What does the speaker of these lines actually *say*? Is it anything so definite as 'I like Chopin's music'? The sentence is vacuous, spoken only to strike an attitude, to make an impression. The imagery is *précieuse*, absurdly pretentious in the metaphor which makes Chopin's music a ' "bloom" ' which is ' "rubbed and questioned in the concert room" '. The rhyming couplet here points up the silliness. This sort of conversation is, we feel, like the room: representative of a culture falling into decadence. The poet expresses his distaste by describing how the conversation 'slips', like something slithery, through other sounds that are themselves muted, enfeebled, as if perceived through sensations that are drugged. The sound of violins (on a record) is 'attenuated', slenderly fading, their music 'Mingled' with 'remote' cornets. The word 'velleities' catches this atmosphere of dulled inertness; wishes and desires are not advanced towards any action. What Eliot renders here, in his imagery and rhythms, is the experience of boredom. Suddenly, though, the languor is interrupted by the Lady beginning her conversation with the poet and we feel a jolt on the brief line 'And begins'.

The Lady's words catch the tone of cultured desperation. They lay a claim to the poet as a particular friend, one who intimately understands and sympathises with the woman. Her long, decorous sentence is an invitation to further intimacy. The Lady expresses her own dissatisfaction with life in an aside which is calculated to flatter the poet into taking on the role of fellow-sufferer. ' "(. . . you knew? you are not blind!/How keen you are!)" '. He is invested with ' "Those qualities upon which friendship lives" ' and threatened with a special place in her affections: ' "How much it means that I say this to you – " '. The Lady's nervous agitation and the suggestion of a neurotic personality are clear even before we get to her final words dramatically dismissing her life as a nightmare: ' "life, what *cauchemar*!" '. The repetitions and hesitations in her speech, the abrupt insistence of ' "How keen you are!" ' all suggest the woman's desperation behind her refinement, a desperation to claim the poet's involvement and sympathy. We sense her boredom, loneliness and fear, as well as the overtly reasonable tones of emotional blackmail.

The closing paragraph shows the poet's reaction. He instinctively resists her advances. In contrast to the cultivated setting of music and conversation, a more primitive, aggressive sensation is felt by him: 'Inside my brain a dull tom-tom begins/Absurdly hammering a prelude of its own.' We feel him wanting to disrupt this mood of menacing politeness, to break through the cultivated artificialities, to express 'one definite "false note" ' amidst the precarious harmonies of the room. Now his tone shifts to a sardonic parody of the life-style of this society: 'Let us take the air, in a tobacco trance' vividly sets before us the atmosphere of fetid staleness, boredom, drugged inertia. The contempt is clinched by the bathetic couplet of 'clocks' and 'bocks'. These lines capture his anger and frustration, but these feelings remain internalised.

The second section takes us forward to spring. Again, the poet is visiting the Lady in her room; on this occasion her conversation is more urgent, more demanding. The poet, though, is fascinated by a grim irony, for as the Lady talks of the abundance of life stretching before him she twists a lilac stalk round one of her fingers. She is more direct in her attempts to solicit his sympathy, hinting at his cruelty and insensitivity. Still, he politely resists: 'I smile, of course,/ And go on drinking tea'. Next, she hints at her ' "buried life" ' of the past and tries to play on his sympathy by contrasting his youth with her old age: ' "I shall sit here, serving tea to friends . . . " '. The poet does not respond except, eventually, by leaving.

There then follows a section of self-reflection. The poet feels guilty for failing to return the Lady's intimacy. Life, action, risk-taking are things he reads about in the papers. It is a drama in which he does not wish to be involved. Instead, 'I keep my countenance,/I remain self-possessed'. The poet fears involvement because it would threaten his own composure. We feel that he has only a precarious grip on his inner life. He preserves his security at the expense of emotional commitment. One senses here the self-discipline of a Puritan rectitude, a resistance to any kind of self-revelation. But there are moments when the self-defensive barriers are penetrated, when sudden longings are unaccountably and intensely felt:

> I remain self-possessed
> Except when a street-piano, mechanical and tired
> Reiterates some worn-out common song
> With the smell of hyacinths across the garden
> Recalling things that other people have desired.

These sudden floods of feeling, associated with and stimulated by such mundanities as a street-piano, are for the poet both irresistible and dismaying. They threaten his self-possession and he does not know what to make of them: 'Are these ideas right or wrong?' At this point in the poem we sense that the Lady's appeals to the poet expose his carefully-shielded vulnerability. He knows the 'things that other people have desired' but does not know whether to join them in their desires. He would be sacrificing his self-preserving detachment for human communality and involvement. Like Prufrock, he is faced with a choice he seems unable to make. It is a choice in which his instinctive withdrawal from human contact is challenged. His austere self-command, although occasionally punctured, is a way of keeping his feelings and emotions in check, subdued. One recalls what Eliot

wrote in an essay about the role in poetry of the artist's personality:·
'But, of course, only those who have personality and emotions know
what it means to want to escape from these things' (*Selected Essays*,
p.21).

The third section recounts a visit to the Lady in October. It is the
poet's final visit for he is shortly to go abroad. As he mounts the stairs
to her room he is assailed by guilt, feeling 'as if I had mounted on my
hands and knees'. Once more, the speaker is ill at ease and the Lady's
words are urbanely accusatory: ' "You will find so much to learn" '.
The poet smiles politely and feels once more inadequate to the
situation: 'My smile falls heavily among the bric-à-brac'. At the
Lady's suggestion that he should write he is instinctively defensive,
unwilling to commit himself in the bartering of emotions. Now the
Lady is more open in her expression of betrayal, wondering why they
have not developed into friends. The poet is utterly incapable of
responding to her, disabled by a self-consciousness which watches the
performance of meekness he is putting on for the Lady. It is as if he
suddenly catches sight of himself in a mirror and sees the act he is
putting on, an act he can barely sustain: 'My self-possession gutters;
we are really in the dark'. The Lady tries her last, pathetic plea as the
emphatic rhymes ('fate . . . rate . . . late') and three-stress rhythm
limp towards the self-pity of ' "I shall sit here, serving tea to
friends" '. The poet keeps up the act in front of her, revealing
nothing of his true feelings of guilt, disgust and a desperation to
escape her presence:

> And I must borrow every changing shape
> To find expression . . . dance, dance
> Like a dancing bear,
> Cry like a parrot, chatter like an ape.

In the final section the poet, now alone, examines his relationship
with the Lady. Has he entirely broken the bonds with her? The
Lady's final words had suggested a continuing involvement – ' "You
will write, at any rate./Perhaps it is not too late" ' – which the poet
may not finally have been able to end. He must continue to indulge
her: 'Let us take the air, in a tobacco trance – '. Now he wonders how
he might feel if she were to die. That explosive first line – 'Well! and
what if she should die some afternoon' – is charged with self-
justification and self-recrimination (you can catch these contrary
feelings by reading the line with the stress either on 'should' or on
'die'). How would he feel if, sitting at his desk with pen in hand,
perhaps about to write to her, he were to hear of her death? All he
can surmise is that he would be 'Doubtful . . . Not knowing what to
feel . . . '. Then the thought occurs that if this were to happen,
'Would she not have the advantage, after all?' Perhaps the Lady

would have once more taken the emotional initiative, forcing him to respond to her, leaving him guiltily justifying his cool behaviour towards her. But at the same time her death would bring their relationship to a conclusion, a gracefully dignified ending, like a muted cadence (a 'dying fall') in a piece of music:

> This music is successful with a 'dying fall'
> Now that we talk of dying –

He does not know how he would react to her death. Perhaps the Lady would have succeeded in forcing him to recognise an attachment between them. But her death might make him finally free of her: her 'dying' would be a ' "dying fall" ' to the balletic manoeuvrings of their relationship, bringing it to a satisfying conclusion. Then, perhaps, he would have succeeded in retaining his self-possession and be released from an unwanted involvement with her. He would have emerged unscathed and victorious: 'And should I have the right to smile?'

The poem's ending, though, remains as an unanswered question. Like Prufrock, the speaker of 'Portrait of a Lady' is by nature timid and self-reflective, caught between attraction and repulsion. In polite society he behaves with self-conscious politeness; when called on, by the Lady, to give something more than politeness he is flustered and unsure of himself. He seems happiest alone, reading of life's dramas in the newspapers, keeping his countenance, remaining self-possessed and self-sufficient. But occasionally he is urgently aware of longings and desires in himself which threaten his self-control. With the Lady, his habit of self-disciplined politeness is threatened, for it is a mask she wants him to drop. He becomes more and more aware of himself as a performer, trying to keep his distance from her without being rude or cruel. He is drawn on by her offers of friendship and intimacy but at the same time is repelled by the vacuities of her social milieu, her neurotic personality, her fear of old age and death, her very need of him. His conscience battles with his own nature: he feels guilty about resisting her but desperate to escape her demands.

The guilt is caught in the poem's epigraph from Christopher Marlowe's play *The Jew of Malta* (c. 1592). The Friar is about to accuse Barabas, the Jew, who quickly interrupts him with a self-accusation which he can then abruptly dismiss – 'And besides, the wench is dead' – so as to pass over the much viler sins that he has just committed. Perhaps the speaker of 'Portrait of a Lady' unwillingly identifies himself with Barabas who is callously explaining away his involvement with a woman in another country who is now dead.

Prufrock, we said, was unnerved by women. He never asked his 'overwhelming question'. He tried to preserve an idealised vision of perfection and beauty by retreating from the real world of sexuality and corrupted flesh. The speaker of 'Portrait of a Lady' is similarly reserved. His is a sensitivity of a particularly aesthetic intensity. The poem is shot through with metaphors drawn from art, music and literature. The very title draws attention to the poem as a *portrait*, an artistic representation of life. The Lady's room is reminiscent of Juliet's tomb and the phrase 'dying fall', with its self-conscious quotation marks in the poem, is taken from Orsino's opening speech in Shakespeare's *Twelfth Night*, itself a speech about music and the unsatisfactoriness of love. The poem proceeds by way of musical images. Voices mingle with the sound of violins whilst the poet feels 'a dull tom-tom . . . hammering a prelude of its own'. The Lady's voice is likened to an out-of-tune violin; her literal death would be like a musical 'dying fall'. It is as if the stuff of human experience is filtered through a sensibility which converts it into the terms of art.

And this may be why the speaker is so solitary, so self-possessed. For him, Art needs to be kept distant from Life if it is not to become tarnished. The speaker must remain aloof, uninvolved, a spectator even of himself (like the one 'who smiles, and turning shall remark/ Suddenly, his expression in a glass'). But there is a high price to be paid in terms of the speaker's loneliness and isolation. More telling, though, is the barely hidden charge of barbarism which the speaker is forced to lay against himself (and hinted at in the epigraph). Not only did he thwart the Lady's expectations of his friendship, he made her the subject of a poem, a poem in which her literal 'dying' is immediately subsumed by the musical metaphor of ' "dying fall" '. Is there not something callous about this conversion, a callousness which surfaces in the last line: 'And should I have the right to smile?'? The man has escaped from the Lady; the poet/artist has finished her off in his poem/portrait.

3.3 'PRELUDES'

The 'Preludes' are the poems of a young man (Eliot was in his early twenties when he wrote them) who is deeply disillusioned, who has seen the emptiness and boredom of life. They present us with city scenes (the first two poems were written while Eliot was a student at Harvard in America, the second two in Paris) in which what is seen – rain, windows, coffee-stands, a woman in a dingy room, crowds leaving work – is made to harmonise with a particular state of mind. The poems are set at different times – evening, morning, night and day – and this sequence helps to emphasise the feeling of dull monotony as if one day simply repeats another day. The title, 'Preludes', can be considered in a number of ways. To what are these evenings and mornings a 'prelude'? Only to repetition, to more and more mornings and evenings in the long and dreary cycle of existence. But the title also points us towards the art of music (where a 'Prelude' is simply a short introductory piece) and there are ways in which these poems attempt some 'musical' effects in their use of rhythm and rhyme.

The poems are snapshots of modern life in the city, what it feels like to be walking through urban streets in the evening or the morning. In the first poem, we are presented with a winter evening which 'settles down' in a way resembling the cat-like fog in 'The Love Song of J. Alfred Prufrock', and we smell evening meals being cooked in cramped lodgings down 'passageways'. A feeling of weary disgust emerges from the image of 'The burnt-out ends of smoky days' (reminiscent of Prufrock's 'butt-ends of my days and ways'). It is raining, and a gust of wind trails 'scraps/Of withered leaves' and bits of newspapers: words like 'grimy scraps', 'withered' and 'vacant' emphasise the speaker's sense of staleness. He hears the insistent beat of the rain and sees at a street-corner a lonely cab-horse, impatient and uncomfortable. Finally, and with a mocking note of drama, the street-lamps are lit to announce the approach of night.

What emerges from the poem, more than its narrative details, is the speaker's mood. He trudges through the wind and rain of a winter's evening and what greets his senses is the detritus of the day: stale smells and discarded newspapers. He is oppressed by the emptiness of it all, the aimless endurance of his own and others' lives. The metre of the poem is monotonously emphatic, with four (and occasionally two) iambic stresses to the line (as if imitating his own trudging pace). The rhymes are equally emphatic, with couplets ('wraps . . . scraps' and 'stamps . . . lamps') surrounding the more complex sequence 'feet . . . lots . . . beat . . . pots . . . street'. The end-stopped lines (that is, we can pause at the end of each line without disrupting the sense) convey the general weariness and only the final line, separated from the rest of the poem, strikes a different note. 'And then the lighting of the lamps' sounds full of dramatic possibilities. But what will the night bring? Only unconsciousness, and then another day.

The second poem brings us to the morning. Just as the evening 'settles down' in the first poem, so now 'The morning comes to consciousness' as if evening and morning have a life of their own to which we are enslaved. Again the feeling is one of oppressiveness. Now we smell the staleness of last night's beer and the streets are trampled by 'muddy feet that press/To early coffee-stands'. Life has become a response to pressure: the pressure of the clock calling us to work and the crowds trudging the streets (Eliot paints a vivid picture of a similar scene in *The Waste Land*). Individual life is submerged in a mass uniformity:

> One thinks of all the hands
> That are raising dingy shades
> In a thousand furnished rooms.

For the poet, this morning activity – the rush to work, the quickly gulped coffee – is a 'masquerade'. It is a performance put on to give life an ostensible meaning and purpose. But what lies behind the performance? If we recognise that this daily routine is an illusion, where are we to find the real purpose of existence?

The third poem switches the scene to a bedroom, where at night a woman dozes fitfully. In the impatient discomfort of a sleepless night, she throws the blanket from her bed and waits for sleep and as she dozes somewhere between sleep and wakefulness her half-conscious mind projects outwards her own interior being, 'The thousand sordid images/Of which your soul was constituted'. What Eliot captures here is that experience of being half-asleep, when the imagination roves at random inside the mind. Like a film on a screen, her dream-images 'flickered against the ceiling' until daylight returns. She hears the sparrows and imagines the street outside: 'You had such a vision of the street/As the street hardly understands'. Sitting on the edge of the bed, she uncurls the papers from her hair (strips of paper were used before the advent of rollers) and drowsily clasps the soles of her feet in her hands.

Again, what this portrait presents us with is the state of mind of the narrator. The woman is unable to sleep, as if the pressures of modern life deny us even that respite. When she does manage to doze, what she experiences is not rest but a nightmarish tangle of images which, 'sordid', reflect the dishevelled quality of her own life. Morning arrives stealthily, creeping up 'between the shutters' like an intruder. The sparrows are singing but, as if to offset the traditionally romantic associations of dawn, Eliot has the sparrows sing 'in the gutters', the last word pointed up by its rhyme with 'shutters'. The general feeling of disgust is intensified in the closing lines. The soles of the woman's feet are an unhealthy 'yellow' and the palms of her hands are 'soiled'. Here is a poem to set alongside all those other poems written throughout the ages, which use the figure of a woman rising at dawn as occasions of celebration. Eliot's poem shows us his version of modern woman: sleepless, guilt-ridden ('sordid images'), addicted to artifice (her hair is unnaturally curled), unhealthy – and alone.

The final poem in the sequence is the one in which the speaker reveals himself most fully. It begins in the third person ('His soul . . . ') but shifts to the first person ('I am moved . . . ') as if the man behind the camera which has taken these snapshots of city life himself steps in front of the lens. The first line tells of strain and tension: in this world of city blocks and the tramping of 'insistent feet' his 'soul' is 'stretched tight across the skies'. His existence is filled only by the passing of empty hours ('four and five and six o'clock'), glimpses of men 'stuffing pipes', the daily routine of evening newspapers, and the confrontation with 'eyes/Assured of certain certainties', assurances and certainties which in truth are insecure. The lives he sees led around him represent 'The conscience of a blackened street/Impatient to assume the world'. What the poet thinks of these lives is obvious: they are 'blackened', blighted, pursuing false values in what the second poem called 'masquerades/ That time resumes'. In an abrupt contrast, the poet suddenly reveals himself:

> I am moved by fancies that are curled
> Around these images, and cling:
> The notion of some infinitely gentle
> Infinitely suffering thing.

But the final section is equally abrupt in its return to cynicism and emptiness:

> The worlds revolve like ancient women
> Gathering fuel in vacant lots.

Life is once again seen as routine drudgery, a struggle for survival amidst depletion and deprivation.

But the quatrain quoted above stands out as a moment of intense pathos. In contrast to the weariness and disgust so prominent in the 'Preludes', these lines have a sudden tenderness. Eliot places them at a dramatically effective moment in the poem. For nine lines we trudge wearily (the tramping of 'insistent feet' is matched by the tramping of the four-stress lines) through the random impressions of ordinary life, an emptiness which threatens the poet. This valueless society, caught in the daily pursuit of empty pleasure and success, is ominously 'Impatient to assume the world'. At the end of the first sentence which builds to this menacing conclusion, the next four lines have a sense of release as the dominant metre is suddenly relaxed. What saves the poet from being engulfed by the emptiness of life is a notion – no more than that – 'of some infinitely gentle/Infinitely suffering thing'. In a poem heavily laden with the particularities of everyday life, here is a moment that moves beyond the material world to something that curls and clings around our ordinary existence: a sense of fragility, beauty, mercy and redemption. It lasts no more than a moment, but this 'notion of some infinitely gentle/ Infinitely suffering thing' is one we might see Eliot pursuing in many of his poems.

3.4 'RHAPSODY ON A WINDY NIGHT'

'Rhapsody on a Windy Night' is similar in many ways to the 'Preludes'. Its setting is Paris: written in 1911 it shows the same disillusionment with contemporary life as the 'Preludes'. The title again refers us to a musical mode, but the emotional enthusiasm and extravagance of rhapsodic music or poetry is, in Eliot's poem, ironically replaced by anxiety and fear. The free-flowing nature of the poem bears some resemblance to music: the occasional rhymes, half-rhymes and assonance and the varied rhythmical units imitate the structure of musical phrases. The structure of the poem is, in fact, carefully controlled; more free-flowing is the progression of imagery as the mind which speaks the poem unravels its states of feeling.

The poem's sections correspond to the successive hours of a night during which the poet walks around the city. Rather than a portrait of a city at night, what we have instead is a portrait of the mind which perceives that city, a mind which comments on what is seen, not explicitly, but by the compaction of unusual images. We begin at midnight when the light from the moon illuminates the street more harmoniously than daylight ('a lunar synthesis'). Just as this light dissolves the normal clear-cut distinctions of daylight, so the poet's mind now moves freely amongst memories and associations, dissolving 'the floors of memory/And all its clear relations,/Its divisions and precisions'. The regularly-placed street lamps seem as the poet walks past them to beat 'like a fatalistic drum' and this sense of looming threat is reinforced by the memories which now, in the darkness, assail the poet, for the memory is shaken 'As a madman shakes a dead geranium'. This startling simile conjures up not a rhapsodic ecstasy, but a sense of dread, of manic grotesque. This nightmarish phantasmagoria continues in the next stanza, when the sputterings of the gas-lamps become a voice directing the poet's attention to a woman (probably a prostitute) who approaches him from a door " 'Which opens on her like a grin' ". Again, the simile is startlingly apt and suggests an imagination which sees malevolence even in the opening of a door. The same thing happens at the end of the stanza, when the corner of the woman's eye (her wrinkles, perhaps) is said to twist " 'like a crooked pin' ". That the image is deliberately far-fetched is precisely its point: just as the moonlight makes these streets unfamiliar, so the imagination has made the familiar frighteningly strange and extraordinary.

From the " 'crooked pin' " of the second stanza we move to the 'twisted things' of the third: a dead branch on a beach and a broken spring in a factory yard. 'The memory throws up' these things in a disordered fashion, for the night has dissolved the normally ordered relation of things. It is as if everything is seen from a new angle: distorted and disproportionate, images are thrown together by implicit association. The world has become 'twisted', dead and inert, like the stiffened branch on a beach or the rusted spring, 'ready to snap', which now surface in the poet's memory. This third stanza not only describes what the poet suddenly remembers: it tells us something of the poetic process ('A crowd of twisted things') and perhaps of the poet's psychological state ('Hard and curled and ready to snap').

The next stanza presents us with a sequence of associations: from a cat licking butter to a child pocketing a toy, to eyes seen in streets, to a crab gripping a stick. It is the rapidly associative process of the memory which links these items together. The stealth of the cat recalls the once-seen stealth of a child, running along a quay, whose hand, 'automatic,/Slipped out and pocketed a toy'. The cat and the child behaved in an 'automatic' way, so automatic that the poet 'could see nothing behind that child's eye'. That mechanical, automatic quality is one the poet has seen all too frequently in the city where people's eyes automatically try 'to peer through lighted shutters'. Like the crab which mechanically grips the end of a stick, humanity has become, in the poet's eyes, a creature of unthinking, unaware, purposeless instinct.

The fifth stanza, the longest of the poem, begins with an unflattering personification of the moon. No longer the traditional goddess of chastity, the moon is now old and dishevelled. Her eye is " 'feeble' ", she has " 'Lost her memory' " and " 'A washed-out smallpox cracks her face' ". She is an old woman, alone, perhaps neurotic (" 'Her hand twists a paper rose' ") and condemned to unvarying routine (" 'the old nocturnal smells/That cross and cross across her brain' "). From this flight of fancy emerge associated reminiscences, each triggering the next: dry geraniums, dust, the smell of chestnuts and 'female smells', cigarettes and cocktails. Just as the moon is condemned to a succession of the same " 'nocturnal smells' ", so the poet is condemned (note the force of the repeated 'And') to relive old memories, to no purpose. And having thus mocked the moon, the poem ends with a final self-mockery. Returning home, the poet prepares for sleep. Everything seems inviting: " 'The little lamp spreads a ring on the stair . . . The bed is open; the tooth-brush hangs on the wall . . . ' ". But the final invitation (" 'sleep, prepare for life' ") is followed by an immediate and grim rejoinder: 'The last twist of the knife'. In a poem of twisted things, this is the last and bleakest. For what the poem has revealed is a mind that perceives only ugliness. Life is empty and meaningless, a routine endurance. What this 'Rhapsody' relates is not the beauty and harmony of life, but the baffling disorder and fragmentary incoherence of existence.

And yet it does so in a marvellously lucid way. Although it brings its parts together in a loose association, the poem has an overall organisation which we might call musical. It has two voices: the voice of the hissing, spluttering gas-lamps accompanying the poet on his journey and directing his attention to the prostitute, the cat, the moon and his own front door; and the poet's own voice which comments on and elaborates further the scenes presented to him by the street-lamps. Although the metre is varied, its iambic regularity imitates the trudge of the poet's step. Like the lamps placed at regular intervals, the metre 'Beats like a fatalistic drum', a beating felt in the repetition of the time ('Twelve o'clock . . . Half-past one . . . ') and in the refrains wherein street-lamps repeatedly 'mutter' and 'sputter'. The use of rhyme, half-rhyme and assonance has the same effect of repetitiousness: the beat of the 'drum' is felt in its rhyme with 'geranium', and the 'gutter/butter' rhyme is echoed in the repeated 'sputtered/muttered' rhyme. Indeed, the most obvious point of the line in French – " 'La lune ne garde aucune rancune' " – lies not in its meaning so much as in its long, melodious sound which is 'hummed' by the lamp. (In fact, the line is a version of two lines from a poem by the French poet Jules Laforgue and means 'The moon harbours no ill-feelings'.) This repetitiousness of sound and metre and the regularity of the poem's structural principle (each stanza following a similar pattern of statement and reflection) express the ennui felt by the poet. Hence, the title is highly ironic, for what is offered is not exalted feeling but weariness and fear. The windy night brings with it the gusts of memories, twisted images and dislocated fragments of which existence seems composed.

3.5 'GERONTION'

'Gerontion' signals a crisis, a spiritual crisis personal to Eliot himself and a cultural crisis he perceives European civilisation to have reached. The old man, Gerontion, who speaks the poem is a symbol both of a civilisation in decay and an individual yearning for spiritual renewal. He is overwhelmed by a sense of futility, degradation and purposelessness, so burdened by a sense of sin and corruption that it seems impossible to communicate with God. The poem is suffused with disgust and despair; although we can feel the same emotions present in 'Prufrock' and 'Portrait of a Lady', in those earlier poems they are kept at bay by the speaker's bitter irony which turns them into scorn and self-mockery. 'Gerontion', however, openly confronts the emptiness of life. The epigraph, from Shakespeare's *Measure for Measure*, imagines life as a state of unconsciousness in which 'youth' and 'age', the beginning and end of life, are only dreams.

The poem is in five sections, each spoken by a frail old man, Gerontion. Through this figure, Eliot depicts Europe itself as a civilisation whose history has brought it to the edge of ruin (the poem was written in 1919). Gerontion's house is 'decayed' and 'draughty', and the second section presents a gallery of European characters caught in ambiguous situations. The third section talks explicitly about the seductive deceptions practised by History. The 'contrived corridors' may refer to the so-called Polish Corridor taken from Germany under the Treaty of Versailles (June 1919) and the 'wilderness of mirrors' in the final section to the Hall of Mirrors in Versailles where the Treaty was signed. Clearly, there is a sense in the poem, particularly in the final images of things being 'whirled' and 'fractured', of imminent doom, impending chaos. Many of Eliot's contemporaries shared the same fear of a collapsing civilisation around the time of the First World War: in 'The Second Coming', for example, the Irish poet W. B. Yeats wrote that 'Things fall apart; the centre cannot hold:/Mere anarchy is loosed upon the world. . . . ' But more urgently than this historical theme, Eliot's poem expresses the need for personal salvation and a fear, close to conviction, that salvation is impossible.

'Gerontion' is the transliteration of a Greek word meaning a little old man. Eliot's persona, the character who speaks the poem, is drawing towards the end of his life. The conditions in which he now lives are seedy, 'a decayed house', 'a draughty house', 'a sleepy corner'. His mind roves, almost randomly, amongst memories, thoughts and feelings which always lead him back to a mood of futility, disgust, despair. There are complex strands of feeling woven together in the poem: a groping towards spiritual consolation in the face of life's purposelessness; a disgust for human sexual appetite and a sense of language itself as something contaminated and incapable of bearing any vital meaning.

The old man is being read to by a boy 'in a dry month . . . waiting for rain' and immediately we recognise the imagery as belonging to *The Waste Land*, to which Eliot originally planned to attach 'Gerontion' as a prelude. The dryness is a condition of sterility that is spiritual and, perhaps in this case, emotional and sexual as well. As the boy reads, the old man reviews his own life (perhaps as a contrast to the heroic passions and dramas the boy is reading about). The old man 'was neither at the hot gates/Nor fought in the warm rain': he was always as he is now, inactive, dulled, old. Indeed, he is as old as European civilisation itself, for 'the hot gates' refers us to Thermopylae (of which the phrase is a literal translation), the site of a notable battle between the Greeks and Persians in 480 BC. Gerontion is thus both an individual old man and the personification of a civilisation in decay. The 'decayed house' is his seedy lodging-house and also Europe itself, exploited by the owner, the 'Jew' who is contemptuously characterised as having been 'Spawned . . . Blistered . . . patched and peeled . . . ' (Eliot later came to regret the flashes of anti-Semitism that he allowed into some of his earlier poems). The conditions in which he lives are barren and squalid. The landscape is bleak: a goat crops a nearby field amongst 'Rocks, moss, stonecrop, iron, merds' and a woman 'keeps the kitchen' and a meagre fire ('the peevish gutter'). The first section of the poem ends with a bleak portrait of Gerontion: 'I an old man,/A dull head among windy spaces', the final line expressing a condition of complete emptiness.

Suddenly, the second section introduces the symbolism of Christianity. ' "We would see a sign!" ' was the cry of the unbelieving Pharisees who called on Christ to prove his divinity by performing a miracle. But rather than a 'sign', we have 'The word within a word, unable to speak a word,/Swaddled with darkness'. This is an expression of Christ's Incarnation which meant a great deal to Eliot. He has extracted the phrase from a Nativity Sermon preached by Bishop Lancelot Andrewes (1555–1626) and Eliot regarded it as one of the 'flashing phrases' which 'never desert the memory' (see his essay on Lancelot Andrewes in *Selected Essays*). Eliot was profoundly affected by the paradox of the Logos, the Word, incarnated in a wordless infant, Christ, who is then pictured as 'the tiger', as in Blake's poem of the same name, springing in 'the juvescence' of the year. But from 'juvescence' (juvenescence, the Spring) we make an abrupt transition to 'depraved May' and an image of the Communion ('To be eaten, to be divided, to be drunk') which then shifts into a catalogue of invented characters all of whom seem sinister. Their names – Italian, French, German – seem to connote a type of cosmopolitan degeneracy. Mr Silvero's 'caressing hands' may be handling Limoges china, or human flesh: Madame de Tornquist may be shifting the candles in the darkened room of a brothel; Fräulein von Kulp may be guiltily startled, caught with one hand on the door. These photographic snatches are never explained and remain as vivid but meaningless recollections in Gerontion's memory. He can make nothing of them: 'Vacant shuttles/Weave the wind' (another image of emptiness).

Why is there a gap between 'Came Christ the tiger' and the following line? It is as if the gap betokens the chasm between the divine and the human, between the Incarnation and the world of human sin. If divinity is 'The word within a word', then how is it to be spoken? 'Christ the tiger' is left to leap across the gap to 'depraved May', and Communion is taken amongst 'whispers', the dishevelled, depraved humanity of Mr Silvero and his kind. This second section seems to wonder whether there is any possibility of knowledge of the divine. Mr Silvero and the rest are surely incapable of recognising 'a sign'; like the Pharisees, they want proof of divinity where only faith will suffice. Being human, they are corrupt, fallen.

The third section dwells on the purposeless workings of human history – purposeless, that is, unless we are prepared to assume a divine purpose for it. The path taken by history is tortuous, deceiving, arbitrary. Caught up in the mindless machinations of history, we are powerless to determine our own destinies. History is a fickle mistress, she 'deceives with whispering ambitions . . . gives when our attention is distracted . . . gives with such supple confusions/That the giving famishes the craving'. What she gives leaves us dissatisfied, or else is given too late when it is undesired. Or else she makes demands of us which are frightening, but 'Neither fear nor courage saves us'. In surveying the blind, accidental, fortuitous, unfortunate twists and turns of history, unpredictable and ungovernable, Eliot/Gerontion is faced with chaos and suffering. We are condemned to be swept up in the onward rush of time, tossed around uncontrollably in its torrent. The passage, with its sequence of sweeping sentences, captures the feeling of rapid movement. It conveys our helplessness, our suffering at the hands of time. The association of history with an untrustworthy courtesan once again links our mortality to a condition of sinfulness. The 'knowledge' of ourselves is the knowledge of our innate sinfulness. The passage closes with a glancing reference in 'the wrath-bearing tree' to the Tree of Knowledge from which Eve stole the forbidden fruit and thus fell into a state of sin. The 'tears' are tears of penitence and the passage is a plea for forgiveness: 'After such knowledge, what forgiveness?' The 'knowledge' is the awareness of our corruption, and particularly (if we recall the Biblical use of 'knowledge' to mean sexual knowledge) of our erotic natures and sexual appetites. If Gerontion, the old man, represents European history, then it is a history of decadence. More profound, though, is the speaker's awareness of himself as one needing to be 'saved'.

In the fourth section, Gerontion tries to make sense of his impending death. He will die when 'The tiger springs', when he is devoured by the tiger, the God of wrath and punishment. But the tiger springs 'in the new year', which suggests the possibility of rebirth. His death may not be 'conclusion': 'Think at last/We have not reached conclusion, when I/Stiffen in a rented house'. His life ('show') may not have been made 'purposelessly'. Then, as if not entirely satisfied or convinced by this approach, Gerontion pauses and tries again: 'I would meet you upon this honestly'. Who is the 'you'? Most obviously, the reader is being addressed directly by Gerontion, an old man trying to explain his life to us. But perhaps we might also read this passage as a continuation of the plea for forgiveness made in the third section. Gerontion, his 'tears' now being shaken, is trying to establish an understanding of God and an unburdening of himself before God: 'I would meet you upon this honestly'. He has been rejected by God, and his former beauty (like that of Lucifer) is now lost in 'terror' (of sin and death) and 'inquisition' (the scrutiny of his own sinful nature). An old man, he has lost 'passion', his capacity for feeling, and indeed may prefer his condition of emptiness ('A dull head among windy spaces') because human 'passion' is bound up with sinfulness, 'adulterated'. But having been rid of his human faculties ('sight, smell, hearing, taste and touch'), how is he now to find God? 'How should I use them for your closer contact?'

The final section poses a question: 'What will the spider do,/ Suspend its operations, will the weevil/Delay?' These may stand as images of human life, the spider weaving its web (the snare of sin), the weevil forever plundering and destroying. Can humanity release itself from sin? The following image, of people 'whirled . . . In fractured atoms', draws upon the classical image of sinners suffering punishment by being hurled into an orbit that carries them away into space. This is the torment of the damned. The verb 'whirled' suddenly conjures up the sense of being tossed about in a storm, hurled by the wind, the wind which has driven Gerontion to his sleepy corner 'in a draughty house/Under a windy knob'. As in the third section, humanity is again seen as powerless, tossed about in a universal maelstrom. We move into a sequence of images picturing a gull resisting a stormy wind (off Belle Isle in the North Atlantic, or the tempests off Cape Horn, or caught in the Trade Winds), its white feathers lost in the snow. This, perhaps, is humankind, flung around and struggling against forces that would hurl it to destruction. Then, as if conscious that these images and ideas are not entirely satisfactory, the poem ends flatly: 'Tenants of the house,/Thoughts of a dry brain in a dry season'. We end as we began, with images of barrenness and sterility. Gerontion must continue to await the rain.

The ending of the poem seems to acknowledge its own unsatisfactoriness. The crisis from which the poem springs remains unspecified. The poem depicts states of sterility, decadence, disgust (mainly figured as a sexual disgust), a consciousness of sin and the need for forgiveness. We might say of this poem, as Eliot said of *Hamlet*, that it 'is full of some stuff that the writer could not drag to light, contemplate, or manipulate into art' (*Selected Essays*, p.144). ('Gerontion' was written at about the same time as Eliot's *Hamlet* essay.) The problem of 'Gerontion' is to find a language by which to express almost inexpressible fears and longings, a language that can hint at divinity. Language is inevitably contaminated, part of our fallen world, and the contamination is felt particularly in the sexual puns and innuendos. Gerontion may 'Stiffen' not only in death, but in copulation, like the 'shuddering Bear'. The 'wilderness of mirrors' may remind us of Sir Epicure Mammon in Jonson's *The Alchemist* (1612) who discourses on the best arrangement of mirrors in which to see his nakedness multiplied. Words like 'Horn' and 'Trades' (prostitution) are used with a deliberate innuendo.

As a poet, Eliot's problem is how to use a contaminated, flawed language to express the search for divine perfection. The 'word within a word' is 'Swaddled with darkness'; as Christ was at the Nativity swaddled in clothes, so the expression of the divine lies obscured in darkness. 'In the juvescence of the year/Came Christ the tiger' ends in abrupt silence and has had to invent a new word for itself ('juvescence'). The poem invents names and words like 'concitation' and even its title, 'Gerontion'. Just as the tears of repentance emerge only with great difficulty (they are 'shaken'), so in this poem Eliot struggles to make a language by which to express a religious yearning that at the time he himself perhaps barely understood.

3.6 'SWEENEY ERECT'

In the early poems such as 'The Love Song of J. Alfred Prufrock' and 'Portrait of a Lady' we found Eliot expressing a point of view not explicitly but by his control of tone and image. In 'Sweeney Erect', Eliot expresses himself even more obliquely, for the poem's 'meaning' emerges only if we are acquainted with some knowledge of classical mythology. More and more, Eliot's scholarly learning itself becomes part of the texture of his poems. His allusiveness – the overt and covert references his poems make to history and literature – has offended some critics: 'a pompous parade of erudition' was not the rudest thing said of *The Waste Land*. But hunting down the source of each and every allusion will not help us to understand why Eliot was drawn to this method of organisation.

The epigraph to 'Sweeney Erect' is taken from *The Maid's Tragedy*, a play by Francis Beaumont (1584–1616) and John Fletcher (1579–1625), at the point when the broken-hearted heroine Aspatia instructs her attendants how to proceed with their tapestry of Ariadne, who in Greek legend had lost her beloved (like Aspatia) and thus stands as her prototype. What the poem immediately establishes for us, then, is a common situation of suffering by women who have been betrayed by men. Eliot's first two stanzas are his continued version of Aspatia's instructions to her maids and the elevated, stylised language imitates the heroic proportions of the classical legend and the Jacobean tragedy. The steady metre, the mellifluous alliteration ('Cast in the unstilled Cyclades'), the elevated vocabulary ('anfractuous . . . insurgent . . . ') all combine to produce a tone of stately gravity.

But this studied rhetoric is immediately mocked by the third stanza which introduces us to Sweeney arising from his bed. Now the classical archetypes are reduced to a parenthetical whisper: Nausicaa, King Alcinous's daughter, discovered Odysseus the morning after he had been shipwrecked and Polypheme figures in a similarly important 'morning' scene in Homer's *Odyssey*. The function of these classical allusions is to guide our attitude to Sweeney. Against this background of high passion, dreadful suffering and heroic endurance, Sweeney intrudes as grotesquely primitive. Eliot's allusiveness is a way of measuring the present and the past. It is not just a matter of his parading his learning, for Eliot's scholarship entered into his sensibility. Nor is it a matter of sentimental nostalgia, of presuming that the past was always better than the present: read in a certain way, Eliot's opening two stanzas are not far short of parody. The allusiveness compresses a range of feelings, a history of suffering by wronged womanhood. Now, in Sweeney, we behold modern man in all his bestial ugliness: 'Gesture of orang-outang/Rises from the sheets in steam'.

By the fourth stanza, we are firmly in the modern age. Ariadne's hair which in the second stanza was tangled by Aeolus's gales has now become 'This withered root of knots of hair' of the girl on Sweeney's bed. The description of her is brief and brutal: she is 'Slitted' and 'gashed', her mouth 'This oval O'. The vocabulary is violent, as violent as the woman's epileptic fit; by contrast, Sweeney calmly prepares to shave and puts the woman's distress down to 'female temperament'. The reference to the American writer Emerson (1803-82) mocks both Emerson and Sweeney. Emerson wrote that 'an institution is the lengthened shadow of one man'; the modern age has produced Sweeney's 'Broadbottomed' silhouette as its representative. While the epileptic shrieks on the bed, Sweeney tests his razor on his leg: the situation is not far removed from the elaborately contrived horrors of Jacobean tragedy (to which Eliot's epigraph referred us).

Now the grotesque comedy deepens. 'The ladies of the corridor' (we are surely in a brothel) are embarrassed by the commotion and, in a perverse distortion of good taste and breeding, 'Call witness to their principles', dismissing the girl's fit as 'hysteria'. While the brothel-keeper mutters darkly, Doris offers succour and aid to the wretched epileptic. Her remedy? 'Sal volatile/And a glass of brandy neat'.

The poem expresses disgust, but the disgust is focussed and controlled by the poem's formal organisation. 'Sweeney Erect' is 'homo erectus', man's upright stance marking his superiority in the animal kingdom. But the title contains an obvious sexual innuendo, for this particular man is in a brothel. Eliot's strict quatrains can in his first two stanzas imitate the rhetorical richness of seventeenth-century dramatic verse and in the rest of the poem take on the clipped ironies of comic verse. The disgust is thus elegantly understated and is to be felt in the contrast between the world of the opening stanzas and the modern world of Sweeney. Eliot's allusions speak of despair and suffering. They are not a romantic yearning for a lost golden age. But they do articulate an intensity of human feeling, whereas Sweeney, modern man, is oblivious and indifferent. Even the presence of the epileptic prostitute does nothing to stimulate our compassion, for she is given to us entirely in terms of physical repulsiveness.

In her own way, she is as horrific as Sweeney. The poem is popul
with monsters who pride themselves on their finer feelings. D
'Enters padding on broad feet': calm and unruffled she brings
simple remedies and the effect is comically grotesque.

If there is disgust in the poem, there is also fear, for Sweeney'
passionless world. But just as the disgust is controlled by E
calculated bathos (in the contrast between the second and
verses), so the fear is subsumed by a dandyish satire. The ve
sprightly, stylish and witty. Nowhere is the horror allowed to surf
no comment is directly made. Our attitude to Sweeney is shap
entirely by the contrast between a grotesque situation and t
elegance with which it is expressed. The neatly end-stopped lines, th
clipped rhythms and rhymes, express a tone of aloof objectivity. It is
the cool, dispassionate gaze of the satirist which clinically describes
the epileptic who 'Curves backward, clutching at her sides'. But
Eliot's allusiveness represents his conviction that there is a scale of
values by which we must judge ourselves. Without the first two
stanzas the poem belongs to Sweeney and his indifference, but the
dense allusiveness of the opening offers us a scale of human feeling
and value by which to measure Sweeney. Allusiveness becomes
Eliot's way of reaching towards moral imperatives and spiritual life.

3.7 'WHISPERS OF IMMORTALITY'

Like 'Sweeney Erect', 'Whispers of Immortality' contrasts two sorts
of sensibility: the seventeenth-century imagination of John Webster
(1580?–1625?) and John Donne (1571?–1631) and its modern counterpart which can only respond to the grossly physical stimulus of
'Grishkin'. Eliot's title, a weakened echo of Wordsworth's 'Intima-
tions of Immortality', suggests that the modern consciousness
chooses only to hear the faintest rustlings of life beyond death.

What Eliot so admired in the work of John Donne, other 'Metaphysical' poets and some seventeenth-century dramatists was their
capacity to blend thought and feeling into a unified sensibility, so that
emotions are felt in the intellect and thought itself has an emotional
impact. The poem's opening line has a lurking ambiguity. Webster
was 'possessed' by death in the sense that it occupied his thinking: but
he was also 'possessed' in a more sensual way, in that the idea of
death was not for him a mental abstraction but a physically immediate reality. Hence Webster saw not a face, but a skull; not eyes, but
daffodil bulbs in eye-sockets. So possessed was he by a sense of death
that in his imagination life was reduced to its fundamental essentials:
dead limbs woven together by the 'lusts and luxuries' of thought.
Donne, too, is celebrated as a man 'Who found no substitute for
sense', who apprehended with a full sensuous responsiveness not only

life, but death (and whose poetry consistently assimilates the act of love with death). He was 'Expert beyond experience': he could perceive reality lying beyond and behind immediate experience. The 'anguish of the marrow/The ague of the skeleton' represents Donne's feverish desire to discover a fundamental reality, a purpose to existence which was not to be satisfied by any 'contact possible to flesh'.

If Webster and Donne were 'much possessed by death', the modern mind is possessed by the fleshly charms of Grishkin, the cosmopolitan seductress. Where Webster saw 'breastless creatures under ground', we now respond to Grishkin's 'promise of pneumatic bliss'. Indeed, the 'mind' is precisely what is absent from these verses, for Grishkin is portrayed entirely in terms of physical sensations and animal lust. Webster's ghastly perception of eye-sockets has its ironic counterpart in Grishkin's eyes being 'underlined for emphasis'; she offers a 'friendly bust', she responds to 'effluence of cat', she exudes a 'feline smell' and is pursued by a 'Brazilian jaguar'. So commanding has her 'charm' become that 'even the Abstract Entities' attend upon her. Thought itself has fallen subject to the physical stimuli of animal urges. Where Donne had a mind that could 'seize and clutch and penetrate', the modern mind can only 'Circumambulate' the flesh. Webster and Donne saw beyond the flesh but the modern mind is entirely caught up in the flesh.

The final two lines release the poet's derision. 'Our lot' (humankind) 'crawls between dry ribs' in being obsessed entirely by the material world represented by Grishkin. The immaterial, incorporeal, spiritual world of 'metaphysics', that world so vividly present to Webster and Donne, is barely penetrated by the modern mind. Engrossed in materiality, we can only 'keep our metaphysics warm', this ironic last line suggesting that at best we have only a feebly abstract idea of death, or of a life after death. What for Webster and Donne was a cause of passionate speculation – the relationship between life and death – has become in the modern age drained and exhausted. Our consciousness of death 'crawls between dry ribs', whereas Webster saw with startling clarity how 'breastless creatures under ground/Leaned backward with a lipless grin'.

3.8 'SWEENEY AMONG THE NIGHTINGALES'

Eliot's avowed intention was to create in 'Sweeney Among the Nightingales' a sense of foreboding. Certainly the mood of indistinct menace is strong, but the poem is not just an exercise in spine-chilling thrills. It is a poem of foreboding – but a foreboding of what?

The nightingales of the title are ambiguous. Nightingales in classical mythology are often associated with blood-sacrifice. In

Sophocles's *Oedipus at Colonus*, the song of the nightingales fills the grove of the Furies which Eliot had in mind as 'the bloody wood' where, at the poem's conclusion, he imagines King Agamemnon hacked to death by his wife. Elsewhere, Ovid's *Metamorphoses* tells of Philomela who, raped by Tereus and mutilated by having her tongue cut out, was eventually transformed into a nightingale. The nightingales conceived by Eliot, then, are not the nightingales of imaginative release and fulfilment addressed by Keats in his 'Ode to a Nightingale'; their presence is altogether darker and more sinister. 'Nightingale' is also a slang term for a prostitute, so that we are immediately, with Sweeney, back in the sleezy world of prostitutes and brothels (the setting may be in South America, suggested by the reference to the River Plate and the Convent of the Sacred Heart which had branches in South America).

With the epigraph – 'Alas, I am struck with a mortal blow' – Eliot puts Sweeney's situation into the framework of Aeschylus's tragedy *Agamemnon* whose dying words these were when he was savagely slaughtered by his wife. But here, Sweeney is once again the 'Apeneck', primitively animalistic, his knees grossly 'spread', his arms hanging down. Outside the brothel are portents of impending disaster: the moon is 'stormy', the constellation of Orion shrouded, the seas 'shrunken'. But, as well as suggesting gloom, these references have mythological associations. 'In the Egyptian calendar, the appearance of Orion forecasts the coming of the harvest rain and the Dog Star the approach of the fertilizing Nile floods' (Southam). So, Eliot's allusions do more than create a sinister setting: they suggest that the harbingers of rebirth and renewal are remote, 'veiled', 'hushed', 'shrunken'. Drifting with the constellation of the Raven is 'Death' and Sweeney guards the 'hornèd gate' which separates the underworld from the world of man. He is already on the brink of the underworld. (More literally, the 'hornèd gate' is simply the entrance to the brothel, if we accept the sexual connotation of 'horned'.)

Inside the brothel is a dulled, fetid atmosphere of drugged lethargy. All is indistinct; individuals are caught in poses of indolence. Somebody 'in the Spanish cape' tries to sit on Sweeney's knee and, having tumbled to the floor, casually 'yawns and draws a stocking up'. A 'silent man in mocha brown' is referred to: he may also be 'The silent vertebrate in brown' and later 'the man with the heavy eyes' who leaves the room to reappear at the window and lean in with 'a golden grin', and indeed this murky figure may be Sweeney himself. But a lurking threat emerges more clearly when one of the girls 'tears at the grapes with murderous paws' and is 'thought to be in league' with 'the lady in the cape'. Declining some sort of 'gambit' (a sexual invitation? a game of cards?) the male figure leaves to reappear outside the window while, surreptitiously and suspiciously, 'The host with someone indistinct/Converses at the door apart'. The nature of the menace is left unclear and is thereby all the more menacing and it is at this moment of greatest tension that we are told that 'The nightingales are singing near/The Convent of the Sacred Heart'.

Here the song of the nightingales is utterly deprived of Keatsian romance and seems instead to portend some approaching catastrophe. For as the last stanza urgently declares, the nightingales also sang when Agamemnon 'cried aloud' as he was butchered and their 'liquid siftings' fell on his 'stiff dishonoured shroud'. The nature of the catastrophe is left unclear but the reference to Agamemnon's murder is suggestive of a terrible death – a death that does not occur literally in the poem, but is everywhere evident in the dehumanised brutishness of the brothel-scene. The sense of obscene degradation is suddenly to be felt in the nightingales' 'liquid siftings' for it is not only their song but also their excrement which 'stain the stiff dishonoured shroud'. Suddenly the picture of Agamemnon's death is one of heartless betrayal – by his wife and by the nightingales who bespatter his shroud with their droppings. This moment of betrayal extends backwards into the poem. As wrong was committed to Agamemnon, so it is committed to human life as it is lived by Sweeney and his companions. What they betray is life itself which is 'dishonoured' by them as Agamemnon's shroud was 'dishonoured' by the nightingales (now the prostitutes). For Sweeney, for modern man, life has become a living death and therein lies the ever-present menace. Sweeney himself is 'struck with a mortal blow' – the blow of a mortality which responds only to mechanical, animal-like relationships and the degradation of love. For Sweeney, the sources of renewal and regeneration are hidden, unavailable to him. He is condemned to a lifeless existence.

The ending of the poem has a tremendous resonance and power as Eliot's fearful horror suddenly blazes. The effect is worked for. The last stanza comes as a climax to a sentence that began in the third stanza and unrolls with mounting power to its conclusion. That conclusion is given a thunderous inevitability by the switch into the past tense as the cycle of betrayal that is human history revolves. As the conclusion of the sentence is delayed, so the note of horror is delayed by stanza after stanza of aloof, ironic detachment. The person who slips from Sweeney's knees to the floor is 'Reorganised' in a coldly automatic way; the man in brown is a 'silent vertebrate' who, like a simple organism, 'Contracts and concentrates, withdraws'. Later 'Branches of wistaria/Circumscribe a golden grin' of the man who leans in at the window: his grin is 'golden' only because of the fillings in his teeth and the word 'Circumscribe' is coldly abstract and comically elevated. The picture offered of human life is one of degradation and sterility. It is death-in-life.

3.9 *THE HOLLOW MEN*

The Hollow Men is a poem of spiritual paradoxes, of impulses and retractions. Its speaker expresses a condition of terrifying emptiness and near-hopelessness. He is an empty shell, a stuffed scarecrow, passively existing in a bleak landscape of cactus and broken stone, or waiting dumbly with his fellow-creatures on the beach of a swollen river. Nevertheless, he is aware of a tormenting paradox in the nature of his condition. For if he is vacant, 'hollow', then he stands ready to be filled. If he knows himself to be nothing, then he may be ready to discover, in the heart of his darkness (the poem's epigraph is taken from Joseph Conrad's novel *Heart of Darkness*) the ultimate illumination and fulfilment. The poem might thus be seen as a turning point between the sterility of *The Waste Land* and the movement towards hope represented by *Ash-Wednesday*. If the upward curve of Eliot's spiritual journey begins with *Ash-Wednesday*, then *The Hollow Men* marks the nadir that is its necessary prelude. Hence we find in the poem a sequence of images and symbols that express this haunting paradox: that the point of utter desolation and hopelessness, once fully confronted and recognised, is the point at which the upward journey might begin. The poem deals with death: the death of an old life, the hoped-for birth of a new. So it is both despairing and hopeful, an awaiting of redemption.

The poem is in five sections, each of them a meditation on the speaker's inner emptiness and his need to find a purpose for an otherwise meaningless existence. Eliot composed them at various intervals over a few years and published them as a complete sequence under the title of *The Hollow Men* in 1925, two years before he entered the Church of England. This method of composition, of bringing together separate fragments to compose a new whole, was increasingly to characterise Eliot's later poems, particularly the *Four Quartets*. What unites these sections is their common mood, the rhythmical inertia of the two-stress metre, and the recurring symbolism of kingdoms, eyes and stars.

Eliot's study of Dante had a profound effect on his spiritual and poetic development and much of the poem's symbolism has its origins in Dante's own poem of spiritual renewal, the *Divine Comedy*. Eliot also draws on other sources, the major ones being the failure of Guy Fawkes's Gunpowder Plot to blow up the Houses of Parliament in 1605 (from which comes the subsidiary epigraph and the image of the 'stuffed men', referring to the straw effigies of Guy Fawkes burned on bonfires each November, and also, perhaps, the 'end' which occurs not with a 'bang' but a 'whimper'); Conrad's *Heart of Darkness* (1902) which itself describes the empty meaninglessness of existence, and Shakespeare's *Julius Caesar*, wherein Brutus describes those 'hollow men' who retreat from decisive action (lines 72–90 in Eliot's poem recall in their phrasing Brutus's speech in II.i., beginning 'Between the acting of a dreadful thing/And the first motion, all the interim is/Like a phantasma', when Brutus broods on his commitment to assassinate Caesar).

Eliot's allusions – and merely to list some of the more obvious sources fails to evoke the shimmering intensity and density of his echoes – universalise his own predicament. His personal situation is made impersonal by an allusiveness which suggests that his own experience has been repeated throughout history. What these sources have in common is the individual's confrontation with inner emptiness and failure, their own blindness and self-deceptions in pursuit of worldly goals.

The first section opens with a simple but paradoxical image: mankind is a collection of 'hollow men' who are at the same time 'stuffed . . . with straw', leaning together like a row of straw dummies. They are incapable of meaningful speech, and their 'dried voices' sounding like 'wind in dry grass/Or rats' feet over broken glass/In our dry cellar' recall the images of aridity in the *The Waste Land*. The isolated couplet (lines 11–12) returns to the opening paradox of the dummies being both 'hollow' and 'stuffed'. Mankind has being, but it is purposeless, unfulfilled, a 'Paralysed force, gesture without motion'. Until man's existence finds purpose and meaning, it remains valueless, inert, 'stuffed' but 'hollow'. Those who with 'direct eyes' have crossed to 'death's other Kingdom' may vaguely remember these lifeless effigies not as active, passionate 'Violent souls' but only as empty, lifeless shells, 'the hollow men'. This closing section (lines 13–18) introduces the symbols of eyes and the kingdoms of death which so preoccupy the poem. Here, the eyes are 'direct', perhaps because they have seen through to the hollowness of life as they cross into 'death's other Kingdom'. This last phrase implies that although the 'direct eyes' have crossed into the other Kingdom of death, the hollow men themselves remain in another domain of death: earthly life itself.

The second section begins by developing the symbolism of the eyes. The speaker fears to meet the eyes 'In death's dream kingdom'. If 'death's other Kingdom' to where in the first section the 'direct eyes' have crossed is death itself, then 'death's dream kingdom' may represent our earthly, mortal existence. We live in a kingdom of death, its 'dream kingdom', because our mortal life is a phantasmal prelude ('dream') to the ultimate reality of death. And so death may be conceived of not as an end, but a beginning; not as nullity, but new life. The 'eyes' the speaker fears to meet in this life do not appear in 'death's other Kingdom'. There the eyes are transfigured into beatitude and serenity: 'Sunlight on a broken column . . . a tree swinging' and 'voices . . . In the wind's singing'. In these lines, the condition of death is imagined as fulfilling and harmonious: shafts of sunlight, the 'distant' and 'solemn' sound of voices caught in a wind which itself sings.

What, then, are the 'eyes' he so fears to meet? The fear is plainly evident in lines 29–38. The speaker begs not to be 'nearer' to this vision. Instead, he will disguise himself as an animal to avoid it (suggesting man's condition as animal-like) or as a scarecrow ('crossed staves') which is blown hither and thither indiscriminately and inconclusively by every passing wind (the scarecrows reminding us of the 'hollow men', also stuffed with straw). The section ends with a frightened plea: 'Not that final meeting/In the twilight kingdom'. The eyes he dare not meet may be human eyes, like the eyes of Beatrice in Dante's *Divine Comedy* when she returns from death to reprove Dante for his infidelity, with eyes of such piercing beauty that he is ashamed to meet her gaze. But these eyes may also represent the judgement of God which will be encountered at 'that final meeting/In the twilight kingdom', the point at which the darkness of earthly life is illuminated by the brightness ('Sunlight') of divine life. What the speaker of this section expresses is both a terror of meeting those eyes and a yearning for the beauty associated with them.

The third section returns us to our mortal existence, 'the dead land', the 'cactus land'. The first verse-paragraph presents a nightmarish picture of a 'dead man's hand' praying to 'stone images' under 'the twinkle of a fading star'. The stone images are false idols of worship, like the 'heap of broken images' in *The Waste Land*. The man praying is spiritually rather than literally dead. The 'fading star' appeared in the beatific vision of the second section but now it is mocked and enfeebled by the word 'twinkle' which recalls the popular nursery rhyme (and nursery rhymes are to recur in the poem's final section). The speaker asks whether it is 'like this/In death's other kingdom' (death itself) and again we feel his yearning to escape from the emptiness and unfulfilment of earthly life, a life during which we wake alone 'At the hour when we are/Trembling with tenderness'. The sexual longing is thwarted; instead, the 'Lips that would kiss/Form prayers to be broken stone'. Such prayers, it seems, are thought of as ineffectual even as they are uttered. This middle section is a portrait of despair. Man is 'dead', praying uselessly to broken images in a parody (hence the deliberate bathos of 'twinkle') of a true quest for salvation, experiencing only loneliness and unfulfilment and doubting the possibility of his redemption.

In the fourth section, we return to the symbol of the eyes and find developed the landscape of section III, the 'dead land'. We are still in the 'dead land', now pictured as a 'hollow valley' of 'dying stars'. This is the condition of our mortal life, 'death's dream kingdom' before 'death's other Kingdom' is entered. The 'eyes' the speaker 'dare not meet' (section II) 'are not here', absent just as they were in the second section. Now, 'There are no eyes here' and the hollow men huddle together 'In this last of meeting places', sightless and dumb on the banks of the 'tumid river'. Mankind is represented as blind, speechless, waiting on the beach of a swollen river it is afraid to cross. This could correspond to the River Acheron which in the *Divine Comedy* flows around Hell and by which the spirits of the damned gather for their crossing into Hell. They inhabit a valley of 'dying stars'; where sections II and III had a 'fading star', now the adjective is significantly altered to suggest something bleaker. Like the men themselves, the valley is 'hollow', a 'broken jaw of our lost kingdoms'. The broken jaw summons up the presence of skulls littering the valley and also suggests their inability to speak.

So this abandoned tribe of men ('lost kingdoms' may suggest their perpetual exile) are 'Sightless', themselves blind but also, since 'The eyes are not here', disregarded by the eyes so feared in the second section. These hollow men lack the vision of the 'direct eyes' who 'crossed' to 'death's other Kingdom'. They are 'the hollow men/The stuffed men' who are remembered, if at all, 'not as lost/Violent souls'. And, lacking vision, they cannot see the eyes which (now in 'death's other Kingdom') have been transformed (in section II) into the beauty of 'Sunlight on a broken column . . . '. They will remain sightless 'unless/The eyes reappear' and allow them to glimpse the higher realm which is presaged by 'death's twilight kingdom'. The eyes that must reappear 'As the perpetual star/Multifoliate rose' may suggest the eyes of judgement so feared (and yearned for) in the second section, where in a kingdom beyond 'death's dream kingdom' they have become merciful. In Dante's *Divine Comedy*, Dante has a vision of the Virgin Mary as a single star and the rose symbolises Mary and the saints gathered in heaven. 'The twilight kingdom', we remember from section II, is the kingdom where mortal life might glimpse and approach the divine life following death. So the 'hollow men' will remain in darkness unless an illuminating vision is granted them, the vision of the life after death. Gathered by the river, they can only hope for a redemption of their emptiness.

The final section begins with a nonsense verse, a garbled version of a children's nursery rhyme. After the dense symbolism of the first four sections, it deliberately strikes a note of absurdity. For that is precisely what the poem has established about mortal life: it is a purposeless absurdity, like the rhyme itself, the manic jocularity of which is felt if you try to say the lines as quickly as possible in order to feel the sudden contrasting stillness of the verses following. The rhyme is traditionally chanted by children as they join hands and skip round in a circle at an ever-increasing speed. Life is thus seen as an endlessly whirling motion, covering distance but arriving nowhere (remember how 'Gerontion' ends with a similar image of whirling, and 'Burnt Norton' uses the same image of circular movement around a still point).

The following three verses summarise the condition of the hollow men. The poem has shown glimpses of a world beyond, a world of divine beauty but one which demands a tremendous act of courage and will to enter (will the 'tumid river' be crossed?). These verses capture the sense of a longing which has not achieved its object. Beginnings are not ended; commencements are incomplete. 'Idea' and 'reality', 'motion' and 'act', 'conception' and 'creation', 'emotion' and 'response' have intervening between them 'the Shadow' – the shadow of doubt, human failing and also, perhaps, the Shadow of the Holy Spirit. And themselves intervening between these verses are isolated phrases, two of them from the Lord's Prayer ('For Thine is the Kingdom, the Power and the Glory'). These phrases are themselves incomplete, broken, abrupt, as if the rest of the prayer is strangled; only the weary line 'Life is very long' stands complete. We may say that this final section is an attempt at prayer, an attempt thwarted by those leaden, abstract verses of doubt and stasis. Finally, three lines (91–3) attempt to blurt out the prayer, and each of the lines breaks off into silence. The section ends as it began, with a garbled verse of a nursery rhyme ('This is the way we clap our hands') and the portentousness of 'This is the way the world ends' is comically deflated by the end: 'Not with a bang but a whimper'. It is the whimper of death, of failed prayer – but also, perhaps, the first sounds of a new-born child, a new life, the Nativity.

The Hollow Men is about life and death, or rather death-in-life and life-in-death. For what the symbolism suggests is that mortal life is a living death if it is not given meaning by a perception of a higher order of existence beyond life and death. Hence death is also a birth, an entry into a higher existence of truth and beauty as temporal life gives way to the eternal. But it requires an act of will, of faith and commitment, to perceive a vision of this eternal life. There are three kingdoms referred to in the poem: 'death's other Kingdom', 'death's dream kingdom' and the 'twilight kingdom', each of them asserting that the kingdom we inhabit in our temporal life is not remote from death, but only one of death's realms. 'Death's other Kingdom' (ennobled by the capital K) is the Kingdom we enter at the end of our mortality; 'death's dream kingdom' is our mortal state of phantasmal awareness and the 'twilight kingdom' is the realm in which the eternal kingdom of brightness might be glimpsed.

Associated with these kingdoms are states of vision. Only those with 'direct eyes', eyes capable of true sight, cross into 'death's other Kingdom' and these, perhaps, are the eyes the speaker of section II 'dare not meet' (and which do not appear) in our mortal realm, 'death's dream kingdom'. They belong to a higher realm, and he begs to avoid them in 'that final meeting/In the twilight kingdom'. He dare not meet them because, being 'direct', the eyes would see into 'his true nature and judge him and he might not escape their glare. But the fourth section calls for the eyes to reappear in 'death's twilight kingdom' 'As the perpetual star', for only by their reappearance can the hope 'Of empty men' be fulfilled. This 'star', in the fourth section, has become 'perpetual'; elsewhere it is 'fading' (as if beyond the speaker's vision) or 'dying'. Now 'perpetual', it is the constant star which gives light to 'the twilight kingdom', the star which illuminates the passage from temporal to eternal existence.

Finally, the symbol of the Kingdom reappears in the closing section where it has been restored to the Lord's Prayer: 'For Thine is the Kingdom'. It is as if the three kingdoms (and the 'lost kingdoms' of section IV) have been assimilated into one, the Kingdom of God, because all these kingdoms are realms ordered and made meaningful by the presence of a divine being. The poem's symbolism thus expresses contraries: that life is death and death is life; that our reality is a dream; that in darkness there is light; in sight there is blindness and that in hollowness there may be fullness. But all this is expressed not as a conviction, but as a hope almost extinguished by doubt. Eliot once wrote that at the highest stage of civilisation man united 'the profoundest scepticism with the deepest faith'. *The Hollow Men* expresses that paradox: that in those most nearly hopeless, hope is most intense.

If the poem represents the beginnings of a turning-point in Eliot's spiritual journey, away from the world-weary bitterness of Prufrock and the despair of *The Waste Land* towards the glimpsed serenity of *Ash-Wednesday* and 'Burnt Norton', it also represents a turning point in Eliot's style. Where earlier poems such as 'The Love Song' surprise by their startling imagery, sudden syntactical variations and shifts of perspective, *The Hollow Men* creates an effect of almost soporific monotony. This is entirely appropriate to its theme of deprivation. The poem is like an incantatory chant. It uses an emphatic two-stress line which occasionally expands but only to return to the two-stress chant. Its imagery circles magnetically around the symbols of eyes, stars and kingdoms. Although there are images of evocative compactness which recall the earlier poems – the 'rats' feet over broken glass' or the scarecrows tossed by the wind – the imagery of *The Hollow Men* draws on the associative power of traditional religious symbols such as the 'Multifoliate rose' and the 'tumid river' of Dante's *Divine Comedy*. The 'ideas' in the poem are conveyed almost entirely through the use of these symbols, as if the 'ideas' inhere in the symbols and cannot be separated from them. Rather than using language to shape and order his experience, Eliot here allows his 'meaning' to flow from images and symbols in a way that often defies rational explanation. The opening of section III, for example, has the suggestive power of a dream or surrealist painting rather than a 'meaning' to be arrived at by paraphrase. The use of rhyme contributes to the incantatory quality of the poem but seems almost accidental rather than calculated for a rhetorical effect. The visionary quality of lines 23–8 is enhanced by the interlinked full-rhymes and elsewhere the rhymes suggest a musical flow to which the absence of formal punctuation largely contributes. 'Poetry begins, I dare say,' wrote Eliot (in *The Use of Poetry & the Use of Criticism*, Faber & Faber, 1964, p.155) 'with a savage beating a drum in a jungle', and the thudding monotone of *The Hollow Men* might be understood in the light of this comment.

3.10 *ASH-WEDNESDAY*

In our reading of 'Gerontion' and *The Hollow Men*, we have been made aware of a terrible spiritual struggle. The earlier poems revealed a sceptical intelligence which looked through the surface of polite social existence to the fear and loneliness beneath and which in *The Waste Land* portrayed contemporary life as a living death. This conviction, that what we choose to call 'life' is a world of death-like insubstantiality, and that reality and truth lie beyond this world, that real 'life' is in 'death', is one that we saw developed in *The Hollow Men*. But this conviction is not one at which Eliot arrived easily. For to say that there lies beyond our ordinary world a higher reality of eternal and absolute truth requires a faith that is always being challenged. Only in rare moments is this eternal order glimpsed. And to pledge one's faith in this higher reality requires a complete and joyful renunciation of the world of ordinary reality, for its pleasures, satisfactions and achievements are now to be understood as illusory mirages in the desert of existence. A proper faith in an immortal reality ('death's other Kingdom') entails an ungrudging attitude of penitential detachment from the things of this world. The penitent renounces the world not with cynicism or bitterness, nor with regret or remorse. What is needed is a state of mind that is utterly accepting, serene and secure. *Ash-Wednesday* is a poem that aspires to this state of mind.

Ash-Wednesday, like *The Hollow Men*, is an assemblage of poems, some of them published previously. Section II had appeared as a poem entitled 'Salutation' in 1927, Section I as 'Perch'io Non Spero' in 1928 and Section III as 'Som de L'Escalina' in 1929. Eliot added to these sections and suppressed their independent titles for their publication as the *Ash-Wednesday* sequence in 1930. The original titles indicate that, like so much else in Eliot's work of this time, the literary origins of *Ash-Wednesday* lie in a reading of Dante and a thrilled responsiveness to the devotional rituals and liturgies of the Catholic Church, and we cannot help but be aware that the writer of the sequence had in 1927 entered the Church of England. In the Church calendar, Ash Wednesday marks the first day of Lent, that period of forty days' penance and fasting which commemorates Christ's temptation in the desert. It is traditionally a time of repentance and in particular for meditating on death: during the Ash Wednesday service the laity are exhorted to 'Remember, O man, that thou art dust, and unto dust thou shalt return'. The six sections of *Ash-Wednesday* may be considered separately as meditations on our ends and beginnings, on the reality that lies beyond our mortal births and deaths. They are attempts at a proper penitence obstructed by doubts, hesitations and feelings of unworthiness that can only be overcome by the grace of divine intercession.

Section I

This opening poem is an attempted affirmation of penitence and an expression of wordly renunciation. Three subsidiary clauses lead to the main statement: 'Because I do not hope to turn again . . . Because I do not hope to know again . . . Because I know that time is always time/And place is always and only place . . . I rejoice that things are as they are'. The opening movement of this section is towards an obedient acceptance by the poet of his inner condition of spiritual limitedness. The first three lines are wearily repetitive; what the poet hopes for is not 'to turn again' to and from the world, to escape the inner turmoil of repeatedly turning to and away from worldly achievement. Now, 'I no longer strive to strive towards such things': he has relinquished worldly ambition, asking himself 'Why should I mourn/The vanished power of the usual reign?' when success is only an 'infirm glory'. But he also accepts that in turning away from the world, he is not going to discover 'The one veritable transitory power', because this 'power' cannot be known in our 'transitory' existence; it lies beyond our temporal world in a place where the poet 'cannot drink . . . where trees flower, and springs flow'. Wherever the poet seeks for it in this world, 'there is nothing again'. He is imprisoned in a state of limiting temporality, where one can only know 'what is actual', the one time and one place that form the boundaries of our existence rather than an immortal state of everlastingness. But now, rather than trying to surmount this truth of the human condition, the poet celebrates it. He gladly embraces his own nothingness, rejects 'the blessed face' and 'the voice', so that from this bedrock of certainty he can joyfully 'construct something/Upon which to rejoice'.

Rather than struggle towards a knowledge of God, the poet must simply and acquiescently await God's mercy. He must give up the argument with himself, must pacify his inner turmoil, 'These matters that with myself I too much discuss/Too much explain'. Instead, he can only offer up prayer: 'Let these words answer/For what is done' and hope for mercy.

In the final paragraph the poet again tries to express the state of mind he hopes to achieve. Because even his own will, his own selfhood, is powerless, like 'wings' which 'beat the air' uselessly, he must be taught 'to care and not to care'. This is the paradox of the penitential condition. He must renounce the world without regret but rather than strive for spiritual knowledge he must await divine intercession. Hence, the poem ends with the words of the prayer to the Virgin Mary which call on her for intercession, the plea she enters to God on our behalf. Before the close, though, we find expressed the hoped-for condition of peace in a language of the most moving simplicity: 'Teach us to sit still'. This line is one that should gather force when you recall the 'fractured atoms' that are 'whirled' at the end of 'Gerontion', as you read of the 'unstilled world' in Section V of *Ash-Wednesday* and as you ponder 'the still point of the turning world' in 'Burnt Norton'. What the poet seeks is a condition of stillness. The past is over and done with. It must be relinquished without regret or cynicism, for that is to put too much value on the past. He must embark on an unknowable future without fear or hope. He must simply await the judgement and mercy of God. Having dismantled the ordinary world of reality, but not daring to hope too much of the future, the poet can rejoice 'that things are as they are' and that he is free now 'to construct something/Upon which to rejoice'. He is free to rejoice at a loss – the worldliness from which he has now detached himself.

Section II

This section was the first of the *Ash-Wednesday* sequence to appear (in 1927) and was originally entitled 'Salutation'. In an obvious sense, the poem is a salutation to the figure of the Lady; Eliot may also have had in mind the moment in Dante's *Vita Nuova* when the poet is welcomed by the Lady 'with a salutation of such virtue that I thought then to see the world of blessedness'. Of all the poems in *Ash-Wednesday*, this is perhaps the most visionary and the one least susceptible to 'explication'. When Eliot was asked to explain the symbolism of the opening line, he simply replied 'I mean, "Lady, three white leopards sat under a juniper-tree"'. We must take Eliot seriously and at his word: the reader must let the symbols and images carry their own emotional impact rather than tease out their 'meaning'.

The opening image is one of destruction. But rather than fear and horror, the feelings it conjures up are of ease and satisfaction, even of light-hearted relief. The 'three white leopards' are reposeful, creatures almost of comfortable docility rather than terror. They have consumed the innards of the speaker whose reference to 'that which had been contained/In the hollow round of my skull' (that is, his brain) sounds self-mocking, as if it were barely worth naming. When God asks 'Shall these bones live?', they are glad ('chirping') to proclaim their newly-achieved beauty: 'We shine with brightness'. They are grateful to 'the goodness of this Lady' and her 'loveliness' who 'honours the Virgin in meditation' and who has brought them to their polished 'brightness'. The poet sees himself 'dissembled' and celebrates it as a condition of purity. His own destruction is a cause of rejoicing ('consequently I rejoice, having to construct something/ Upon which to rejoice').

The Lady 'in meditation' is remote from the bones, and the poet himself seeks a similar state of absorbed distraction: he will 'proffer my deeds to oblivion'. For only thus can he 'recover' himself. As the Lady is 'withdrawn . . . to contemplation', so the poet would forget himself, 'concentrated in purpose'. The bones have been glorified by the body's dismemberment. It is as if only by having reduced himself to nothingness can the poet achieve the rapt contemplation exemplified for him by the Lady. The bones achieve true life by being dismembered one from another. As portrayed in this image, death is the way to true life, and to emulate the Lady's contemplative serenity (she is clothed in a white gown) the individual must relinquish entirely his hold on mortal life: 'As I am forgotten/And would be forgotten, so I would forget'. The whiteness of the bones declares the purity of death: 'There is no life in them'.

Hence the bones' song ('burden') is a litany of praise to the Lady. The song is a 'prophecy', but one that goes unheard in the world, 'for only/The wind will listen'. It is a litany of paradoxes in imitation of the Roman Catholic Litany to the Blessed Virgin Mary and circles around the symbols of the Rose and the Garden (both of which have Biblical associations with the Virgin). The symbol of the Garden is one that has particular prominence in *Ash-Wednesday* and 'Burnt Norton', and the litany ends: 'Grace to the Mother/For the Garden/ Where all love ends' so that the female figure is indissolubly linked with the fertility of the Garden.

The final paragraph returns to the opening symbols. The bones 'are glad to be scattered, we did little good to each other'. Any hint of irony here is undercut by the phrase 'the blessing of sand'. The desert, an image of such horrifying aridity in *The Waste Land*, is here accepted gratefully. The bones can, in the desert, forget themselves 'and each other, united/In the quiet of the desert'. This is the world of actuality; as in Section I when the poet rejoiced 'that things are as they are', so here he accepts that 'This is the land. We have our inheritance'. The recognition of earthly reality is here neither grudging nor bitter. If *The Waste Land* was for Eliot a piece of rhythmical grumbling, *Ash-Wednesday* shows him to have ceased grumbling.

Worldly reality is not to be evaded or railed against. It is to be accepted as our providential condition, for 'the desert' might yet be redeemed by 'the Garden'.

Section III

The third poem of the sequence portrays the temptations which impede the speaker's spiritual progress. The image of the spiralling stairs obviously suggests the movement of ascent whether or not we are aware of its echo of Dante. As the speaker climbs upwards, he turns and sees below a 'shape' which is 'Struggling with the devil of the stairs' and the speaker seems to recognise it as 'the same' as his own shape. It is struggling with the devil 'who wears/The deceitful face of hope and of despair'. What the speaker sees is his own internal battle, the tortured state of his inner arguments and debates, the conflict between his scepticism and his faith referred to in Section I as 'These matters that with myself I too much discuss/Too much explain', and which now recurs 'in the fetid air' signifying its staleness. He must not be distracted by the fruitless workings of his own intellect but instead set himself to continue his climb. He leaves the figures behind him, but in the second section must confront the blank darkness ahead of him. What he faces is emptiness and a sense of disgust and decay, 'like an old man's mouth drivelling'. Again, the speaker must surmount this sense of his own repulsive meaninglessness.

At the next stage of the journey occurs a vision of enchanting loveliness. Through a slotted window is glimpsed a scene of inviting beauty. Beyond 'hawthorn blossom and a pasture scene' is a figure who 'Enchanted the maytime with an antique flute'. Now the speaker's imagination begins to wander to the scene outside, drawn by sensuous fantasies of 'brown hair over the mouth blown'. Suddenly, these long, luxurious lines are pulled up short by the peremptoriness of 'Distraction, music of the flute, stops and steps of the mind' as the speaker's mind recollects itself and resumes its journey with a 'strength beyond hope and despair'. For a long moment, the speaker was entranced by beauty and pleasure imagined as a female figure playing a flute in a summer landscape. It is an 'Enchanted' moment, but that adjective suggests a dangerous illusoriness. Nevertheless, the strength required to resist this distraction is a strength that can only come from God, as the closing prayer indicates.

These three visions represent allegorically three temptations that impede the speaker's spiritual journey. The first is the temptation to self-absorption, a self-scrutiny that distracts from a knowledge of God. The second temptation is self-disgust, a sense of weariness and futility which is close to despair. The third is self-indulgence, when the will is sapped by the imagination's craving for earthly beauty and fulfilment. To surmount these temptations, the speaker needs divine intercession to help him in his journey.

Section IV

This poem and the two following are brought into unity by the common features they share. There is the constant presence in them of the Lady figure who resembles the Virgin Mary (but who is also connected with Beatrice in Dante's *Divine Comedy*). Images of the desert and the garden recur more frequently in these final poems. Stylistically, they resemble each other too in a rhythmical relaxation whereby the lines are now more supple and fluid.

The fourth poem is a vision of redemption. The opening movement (up to 'Sovegna vos') portrays a mysterious female figure 'in Mary's colour' who seems to bestow grace and beauty. She resembles the Lady of Section II who was addressed by a Litany of paradoxical attributes: now she is 'In ignorance and in knowledge of eternal dolour'. She restores strength and freshness and beatifies a desert landscape: 'Made cool the dry rock and made firm the sand'. The colours associated with her (violet, white and blue) make her symbolic of intercession. The plea is that she be mindful of us ('Sovegna vos' are the words of Arnaut Daniel to Dante, asking him to remember Daniel's suffering for his lust).

This figure of gentleness and mercy belongs to the speaker's earlier life. The years between then and now, 'the years that walk between', are dismissed and in their stead is restored this dream-figure ('who moves in the time between sleep and waking'). Like a flower in its petals, she wears 'White light folded, sheathed about her'. Because of the presence of this figure, the years of 'the fiddles and the flutes' which were otherwise purposeless are now given value and meaning. She is restorative and the plea is that she will 'Redeem/The Time', that human existence be made meaningful by her grace and that she will make real 'The unread vision in the higher dream'.

As if in answer to this plea, 'the silent sister' seems to assent. Amongst the yews (symbolic of death) and behind the god of fertility (Priapus, or Pan) whose flute is silent, it is only at her sign that 'the fountain sprang up and the bird sang down'. She is 'The token of the word unheard, unspoken'; as the Virgin Mary, she is the figure of Incarnation, of God made flesh. She redeems human history by accepting to become Mother of God; the closing phrase reminds us of the prayer which ends 'and after this our exile show unto us the blessed fruit of thy womb, Jesus'.

Section V

By contrast, Section V presents us with a condition in which mercy and grace are absent. If, in the words of St John, 'He was in the world and the world knew him not', then Section IV may be said to dwell on the first half of John's phrase and this Section on the latter. The opening paragraph speculates on the presence of the unheard Word by way of its obsessive repetition of 'Word . . . word . . . World . . . world' culminating in the homophone of 'world . . . whirled'. This is the condition of the unredeemed world: purposeless change and movement, a constant alteration caught in the ugly repetition of sounds in this first section which is itself imitative of a whirling motion (like the close of 'Gerontion'). In contrast to all this is the single word 'Still' to describe the 'unspoken word', the incipience of God. It is a quality which Eliot constantly returns to in his Christian poems: the first Section of *Ash-Wednesday* implored that we be taught to 'sit still' and 'Burnt Norton' meditates on the significance of stillness.

The poem goes on to describe the condition of the world in which the 'Word is unheard. Again, the clamorous rhymes imitate the cacophony of the world where 'there is not enough silence' for 'the voice' to be heard. The final paragraphs reveal the need for divine intercession. The 'veiled sister' must pray for those 'who chose thee and oppose thee', who are torn between faith and doubt, hope and despair, like 'children at the gate/Who will not go away and cannot pray'. The speaker is one of those who 'affirm before the world and deny between the rocks' and for whom the garden is succeeded by 'the desert/Of drouth'. We are back in the waste land.

Section VI

This final section brings together the hopes and fears of the previous two poems in serene reconciliation. We return to Section I, but now 'Because' has become 'Although'. What is implied in the change is a sense of acceptance, and what the speaker accepts is his own uncertainty and vacillation. He recognises his own 'Wavering between the profit and the loss'. Life is a 'brief transit', a 'dreamcrossed twilight'. And 'though I do not wish to wish these things', nevertheless he is drawn towards the fulfilment of earthly desires, symbolised in the imagery of a seascape (recalling the close of *The Waste Land*). He cannot entirely resist the goodness of the world and the senses: 'And smell renews the salt savour of the sandy earth'. Human existence is 'the time of tension between dying and birth': the inversion of the expected order of 'birth . . . dying' suggests that death-as-birth is now a matter of conviction for the poet. The notion of death is present in the symbol of the yew-trees (so often to be found in graveyards) which are now symbolic of life. For when the will wavers, 'when the voices shaken from the yew-tree drift away', another 'yew' will take up the prayer and resolution will return.

We end with a final invocation to the 'Blessed sister', the 'spirit of the garden'. Again she must 'Teach us to care and not to care/Teach us to sit still' among the rocks of the deserts and we can only trust to 'Our peace in His will'. Divine mercy and blessing cannot be fully experienced in this world, only awaited in the next. As a penitential exercise, *Ash-Wednesday* ends in an acceptance of the human condition.

3.11 'JOURNEY OF THE MAGI'

In 1927 the publisher Geoffrey Faber asked Eliot to write one in a series of poems published in the form of an illustrated text for Christmas. These poems are now gathered under the title of 'Ariel' poems, of which the first is 'Journey of the Magi'. The Magi were the three kings or wise men – Balthazar, Gaspar and Melchior – who according to Matthew's gospel came from the east to pay homage to the new-born Jesus. The story of the Nativity and the wise men is sufficiently well-known and Eliot found a more precise framework for his poem in a sermon preached by the seventeenth-century divine Lancelot Andrewes on Christmas Day 1622: 'A cold coming they had of it at this time of year, just the worst time of year to take a journey, and especially a long journey in. The ways deep, the weather sharp, the days short, the sun furthest off . . . '. Eliot's poem is an occasion for him to use the imagined narrative spoken by one of the Magi as a parallel commentary on his own tortuous spiritual journey.

As in *The Hollow Men* and *Ash-Wednesday* (whose constituent poems were composed between 1924 and 1929), 'Journey of the Magi' seems to be spoken by a single voice which narrates its experience. The opening sentence, in quotation marks, abbreviates the section of Andrewes's sermon quoted above. In an act of sympathetic identification, Eliot continues with the magus's story, for in a way the magus's story is also his own. The Magi underwent a difficult and painful journey which entailed their giving up old comforts in order to witness a Birth that 'was hard and bitter agony for us'. The wise men achieved their objective – but not without awesome cost.

In 'The very dead of winter', the Magi travelled to find new life. But the journey was a long struggle: there were times when the Magi yearned for the old luxuries they had forsaken and were assailed by doubt 'With the voices singing in our ears, saying/That this was all folly'. Finally, after fruitless searching, they arrived at the birth 'not a moment too soon': 'it was (you may say) satisfactory'. Now the speaker looks back on his experience, but not without qualification. 'I would do it again', but the speaker urgently insists that his reservations be noted: 'were we led all that way for/Birth or Death?' For the birth that he witnessed was also a death and having afterwards returned to his kingdom the magus is 'no longer at ease here, in the old dispensation' and yearns for 'another death'.

The magus's narrative is clearly analogous to what Eliot perceived as his own spiritual condition. The birth of Christ was, for the Magi, also a moment of death: the death of an old way of life. As we find elsewhere in other poems of this period, Eliot is here pondering the agonising paradox involved in religious faith: that to embark on a new spiritual life is to extinguish the old life, that before Birth there must be Death. The hardship of the Magi's journey represents the sacrifice they must make as a prelude to Christ's birth. The camels are 'refractory', and this strangely abstract word calls attention to the stubborn unwillingness in himself that the spiritual pilgrim must overcome. There is regret for what must be relinquished: 'The summer palaces on slopes, the terraces,/And the silken girls bringing sherbet', and these are presented unambiguously by Eliot as exerting the genuine attractions of the old way of life. They are not to be easily overcome, especially when the spiritual journey is so full of diffi- culties, the tortuous strain felt in the drawn-out sequence 'And . . . And . . . And . . . '. Finally, the Magi must travel by night, always in darkness. That is their inevitable condition, for the cities are hostile 'and the towns unfriendly' in a disbelieving world where the 'night-fires' – moments of spiritual conviction – are always 'going out'. This journey is undertaken in the full consciousness of doubt. The 'voices singing in our ears' are not angelic acclamations; on the contrary, the last line is flatly convincing: ' . . . this was all folly'.

The central section leads towards the Nativity by way of ambiguous symbolism. It is 'dawn', the valley is fruitful, 'smelling of vegetation', and water runs freely. If these symbols are suggestive of an approach- ing regeneration, they are abruptly challenged by the 'three trees' reminiscent of the three crosses at Christ's crucifixion. The 'white horse' in the meadow may be a reference to the Biblical account of Christ as conqueror riding on a white horse but this horse 'galloped away'. The Magi call at a tavern where men are 'dicing for pieces of silver' and what is called to mind is the betrayal of Christ for thirty pieces of silver by Judas and the soldiers at Christ's crucifixion dicing for his robes. These symbols, by foreshadowing Christ's crucifixion whilst simultaneously preluding the Nativity, state the poem's central crux of the interrelatedness of Birth and Death. Christ's death became inevitable at the moment of his incarnation as his crucifixion heralded eternal life. But the most extraordinary moment in the poem comes with the Magi's arrival at the birth. There is no sense of immediate wonder or celebration: only the matter-of-fact reticence of 'it was (you may say) satisfactory'.

In the final section, the magus tries to fathom the significance of what he saw: 'were we led all that way for/Birth or Death?'. Birth, in its capitalised form, is the literal birth of Christ but also the Birth of a new spiritual life. But that Birth brought with it a Death – the death of the old life, old ways of living and feeling. He had thought that birth and death 'were different' but 'this Birth was/Hard and bitter agony for us, like Death, our death'. So the Magi return, but only to a life of estrangement. They must continue to live 'in the old dispensation', for the new dispensation will come only with that 'knowledge in the mystery of Christ' described by St Paul. The Magi remain amongst 'an alien people clutching their gods', the false idols of the old life. Before entering on the new life, another death is required, as Christ's was. So the magus concludes by accepting the paradox: 'I should be glad of another death'. Death is something for which the magus now yearns, for only by his own death will he achieve new life.

Eliot achieves in his poem the expression of a religious state of mind. It does not assert belief, but the readiness to believe, the sense of its impending inevitability. It is not celebratory but humble. Eliot manages to capture the magnificent plainness of Lancelot Andrewes's prose. In the Christmas Day sermon already referred to, Andrewes wonders what wisdom the Magi – the wise men – might have discovered at the Nativity: 'No sight to comfort them, nor a word for which they any whit the wiser; nothing worth their travel . . . Well, they will take Him as they find Him, and all this notwithstanding, worship Him for all that' (quoted in Southam, p.122).

3.12 'BURNT NORTON'

Like *Ash-Wednesday*, the sequence of poems constituting *Four Quartets* was written over a period of several years and only later did Eliot come to see them as composing a unity. The first poem, 'Burnt Norton', was published separately in 1935; 'East Coker' was published in 1940, 'The Dry Salvages' in 1941 and 'Little Gidding' in 1942. Each of the poems takes its title from places which for Eliot held powerful associations. Burnt Norton is the name of a house near the village of Chipping Camden in the Cotswolds (a country area in central England); East Coker is the Somerset village which Eliot's forebears left in the seventeenth century to go to America and which Eliot visited in 1937; 'The Dry Salvages' refers to a group of rocks off the Massachusetts coast beloved by Eliot from his boyhood sailing trips, and Little Gidding marks the site near Huntingdon of a seventeenth-century Anglican community commemorated by a chapel which Eliot visited. Although we cannot avoid the intensely intellectual quality of the poems – we might think of them as quests for the experience of those absolute truths proposed by Christian theology – we should remember that the poems grew out of the emotional response to particular places and that they were written amidst the fears, tensions and deprivations of war-time England. At a time when all civilised values were threatened and chaos loomed, the poems represent a search for those moments of timeless perfection and fulfilment in human life. They blend the search for aesthetic perfection with the search for religious truth.

Eliot's eventual collective title for the poems – *Four Quartets* – invites us to think of musical analogies for them. We might do this in two ways, by considering *structure* and *theme*. A classical quartet – a musical composition for four voices or instruments – is constructed on principles of formal organisation whereby a number of themes recur, transposed into varying keys, given to different instruments or altered by inversions and variations. We find the same sort of organisation in the *Four Quartets*. Each poem is in five sections. The first section of each dwells on the theme of time. The second sections comprise a lyric followed by a more discursively philosophical passage. In the third sections recur images of journeying (itself connected with the idea of time). The fourth sections, all of them brief, suggest moments of divine intercession and the fifth sections turn to ideas about art to find analogies for Eliot's spiritual quest.

What matters is not that you know the details of Eliot's pattern in the *Four Quartets* but that you understand his basic procedure. Let us say that the fundamental theme of the *Four Quartets* is time. Time is the medium in which we have our existence and we experience it as a constant flow of successive moments. If the opposite of time is timelessness, or eternity, then it follows that eternity is not a condition of never-ending time (for endless time is not the opposite of time but only time extending beyond the grasp of calculation) but *stillness*, a perpetual state of unchangingness. Eliot's spiritual quest is to locate in human life these moments of stillness, when it seems as if the divine realm of eternity momentarily intersects with our mortal realm of temporal linearity and passage. In such moments, Eliot seems to suggest, we experience a moment of divine fulfilment and harmony and glimpse the presence of divine love. But such moments come unlooked for; they cannot be anticipated or summoned up and they occur without warning. To some people, perhaps most, they might never occur at all; to others, including Eliot, they are the most important moments in life:

Why, for all of us, out of all that we have heard, seen, felt in a lifetime, do certain images recur, charged with emotion, rather than others? The song of one bird, the leap of one fish, at a particular place and time, the scent of one flower, an old woman on, a German mountain path, six ruffians seen through an open window playing cards at night at a small French railway junction where there was a water-mill: such memories may have symbolic value, but of what we cannot tell, for they come to represent the depths of feeling into which we cannot peer. (*The Use of Poetry & the Use of Criticism*, p.148).

I have taken this passage entirely out of context and am in danger of misrepresenting it, but I think it helps us to approach an understanding of Eliot's quest for these timeless moments, for that sudden sense of being lifted out of time.

But all this is merely to outline the 'theme' of the poems. The musical analogy to which Eliot's title points suggests the way in which this theme is handled. Like a theme (or 'motif') in music, it is constantly present as a reference point, but always approached and stated in different ways, modified and developed with different harmonies and colourings as a musical theme is articulated. With a poem as notoriously difficult as 'Burnt Norton', it may help to draw back occasionally from expository explanation to consider what its overall title most obviously asks us to consider: its *musical* effects.

We begin the first section with an announcement of the major theme of the piece, the theme of time. The meaning of the lines is knotty and complex, but the heavy four-stress metre ('Time present and time past/Are both perhaps present in time future') has a stately gravity, like the even-paced measure with which the opening theme might be announced in a piece of music. (And so at the end of this first passage we might think of the separated lines ('But to what purpose . . . I do not know') as acting as a short transitional link to the next passage about the garden.)

The opening sentences dwell on the concept of present time containing both past time and future time. The present moment is an accumulation of all the past moments which led up to and created this present so that we might say that the present has been 'contained', stored up, in the past. This present was once the future, so that it is then equally true to say that the future is contained in the past. In fact, our ordinary division of time into past, present and future falsifies our real experience of time as a continuous present which contains both past and future: the past because what we are is the sum of what we have been and the future because what we shall be is fashioned by what we are and have been. Hence, 'If all time is eternally present/All time is unredeemable' because we cannot change past, present or future. All we can do is speculate about the 'What might have been' which exists alongside 'What has been'. At any given point in our lives we might have chosen and acted differently and this is as much a part of our past as what we in fact decided. So the present is composed of both 'What might have been and what has been' and our imaginations are free to explore 'What might have been': 'Footfalls echo in the memory/Down the passage which we did not take . . .'. And so the rose-garden into which Eliot's poem takes us is an occasion of 'What might have been' which is just as much a part of him as 'What has been'. The rose-garden represents an imagined – *and hence real* – moment of transfiguration, when for an instant the world appeared renewed, and an intensity of experience occurred such as seems to belong to a moment of stillness lifted above the relentless sequence of time's passage.

Two biographical notes might be adduced which simplify and clarify Eliot's rose-garden. On a visit to his birthplace late in his life, Eliot recalled the wall which separated his garden from a schoolyard and beyond which he could hear the voices of the schoolgirls, but not see them. 'But there was a door in the wall, and a key. When the girls had left in the afternoon, the little boy would sometimes open the door and enter the yard. He remembered an ailanthus tree within it. Occasionally, he would wander through the corridors of the deserted school. But once he arrived too soon, and the girls were staring at him through a window. And he fled.' (Ackroyd, p.22). Images of the door and the sound of children's laughter in 'Burnt Norton' may owe something to this childhood memory. The second biographical occasion is Eliot's visit in 1934 to the garden of Burnt Norton with his American friend, Emily Hale, to whom Eliot was very attached.

The rose-garden is 'our first world'. It is full of hidden presences – voices, eyes, birds – which are welcoming rather than threatening. We stare into a drained pool, dry and brown-edged, which is suddenly and mysteriously 'filled with water out of sunlight,/And the lotus rose, quietly, quietly,/The surface glittered out of heart of light'. This moment, with its image of intense light, resembles the encounter with the hyacinth-girl in *The Waste Land* ('I knew nothing,/Looking into the heart of light, the silence') and the vision of the Lady figure with 'White light folded, sheathed about her' in *Ash-Wednesday*. Characterising these moments is a sense of vivid illumination, a brief glimpse through the surface of daily life to the reality beneath. But it can only be glimpsed: immediately, 'Go, go, go, said the bird: human kind/Cannot bear very much reality'. As the vision fades, the closing lines quietly return to the opening theme: all we can usually know is a continuous present composed of both what has happened in the past and, existing 'in a world of speculation', what might have been.

The lyrical opening of the second section introduces a new 'tone' into the music of 'Burnt Norton' and a new rhythm with its regular iambs (a light stress followed by a heavy stress) before we are returned to a more prosaic, discursive style by what follows. The lyric passage throws together all sorts of opposites and contraries so as to say that the ever-changing flux of experience, composed of so many disparate elements, in reality composes a pattern, a harmonious completeness. The opening image of 'Garlic and sapphires in the mud' contains an enormous variety of contrary impressions: the precious and the valueless, weight and lightness, dullness and glitter, softness and hardness (you should be able to add to this list). They 'Clot' the roots of the tree, and the idea of sap easily leads on to the idea of blood in the human body: 'The dance along the artery'. There is perpetual movement within our bodies, an endless flux which we see mirrored in the movement of the stars and planets. We are aware of light dancing on a leaf and we hear the pursuit of boar by boarhound. All is movement, transition, change, but there is within it all a unifying pattern as when human movement is composed into a dance. But in order to perceive the pattern, we must see it from a particular point of view, a point of stillness within the movement. So the second half of this section goes on to meditate on 'the still point of the turning world'.

'The still point' is the object of Eliot's search. Hinted at in *Ash-Wednesday* ('Teach us to sit still'), in 'Burnt Norton' it describes an attitude to existence by which a meaning and purpose in life might be perceived. The Greek philosopher Heraclitus (from whom the epigraphs to *Four Quartets* are drawn) proposed that existence is a perpetual state of flux and change, ultimately between being and non-being. We experience this flux in the constant process of time. If we are entirely caught up in this flux, we cannot perceive it as a pattern. But very occasionally we might be granted those visionary moments when we are lifted beyond time to a moment of stillness or 'eternity' in which the whole of life is suddenly perceived as having beauty and meaning. This moment cannot be truly defined except by negatives: it is neither 'Flesh nor fleshless', 'arrest nor movement'. Such moments cannot be borne for long because our 'changing body' has 'woven' into it an 'enchainment of past and future' which protects it from perceiving too long the ultimate realities of 'heaven and damnation' ('human kind/Cannot bear very much reality' we read in Section I). When we live in time, caught up in the flux, we are not truly 'conscious', for 'To be conscious is not to be in time'. But only in our time-bound existence can we occasionally reach the moment beyond time, 'the moment in the rose-garden', when we achieve a stillness beyond the flux. We cannot escape time: we must endure it in the knowledge that the flux does compose an ultimate pattern: 'Only through time time is conquered'.

The second epigraph from Heraclitus speaks of 'the way up' and 'the way down'. What Heraclitus suggested was that spiritual truth can be reached either by a full response to the created world ('the way up') or by its opposite, a completeness of self-denial and a deprivation of the senses ('the way down'). The third section of

'Burnt Norton' follows 'the way down'. In doing so, it uses images drawn from the London Underground and makes of it a kind of Hades in which the tortures of the spiritually unenlightened are depicted. Here, in the Underground station, is neither daylight nor darkness, neither 'the way up' nor 'the way down'. Faces are 'time-ridden', strained by their enchainment to flux rather than stillness (these faces are perpetually travelling on a journey, never still). They are 'empty of meaning', 'whirled by the cold wind' of time's passage ('whirled' reminds us of its similar import in *Ash-Wednesday* and 'Gerontion'). These men are no more than 'bits of paper' tossed about in the 'faded air'. This picture of meaningless existence is of a 'twittering world', not the true 'darkness' or silence of spiritual aspiration.

Hence we must 'descend lower' to the world of 'perpetual solitude' and 'Internal darkness', a world in which we achieve stillness by depriving ourselves of all responsiveness. This is 'one way', the way downwards, towards stillness; 'the other', the way upwards, 'Is the same' because both achieve an 'abstention from movement'. But the world is forever driven on by its longings and desires ('appetency'), condemned to an objectiveless journey 'on its metalled ways/Of time past and time future'. The 'metalled ways' are the tracks of the Underground trains, forever travelling but never arriving.

Section IV is another lyric of sensuous fullness. It is twilight and we are once again in the garden. There is a sense of waiting and expectancy and what is felt is the imminent presence of life and death. As coolness follows the heat of day the poet wonders whether he will be touched by the beauty of life – the sunflower and clematis – or the colder grip of death, the 'Fingers of yew'. (Notice how typographically the poem shrinks to the single word 'Chill'.) In this mood of heightened anticipation, a moment of stillness is achieved and in the recollected image of a kingfisher's glittering wing we are once again presented with a moment suffused with silence, brightness and stillness: 'the still point of the turning world'.

In the concluding poem, Eliot turns to a consideration of his own endeavours as an artist and finds a unity between his artistic and spiritual aspirations. Like sounds in a piece of music, words in a poem only make sense successively, when one follows another in proper order. They 'move' in sequence, just as one moment follows another in time. Like everything else subject to the flow of time, words 'die' and are succeeded by silence. 'Burnt Norton' has presented us with the experience of timelessness, or stillness, when the seemingly random nature of change and flux is suddenly seen to fall into a pattern. This, says Eliot, is also what happens to words in a poem: their patterning, their placing, gives them a meaning that is fixed. (So, for example, the word 'lie' is given its meaning – to lie down or to dissemble or both meanings simultaneously – only according to its place in a sequence of other words.) It is by 'the form, the pattern' that words or music reach a 'movement' that is also 'stillness'. By this, Eliot does not simply mean long-lastingness, as a violin might hold a note for a long time. He means 'co-existence': a state in which the beginning is contained in the end and the end in the beginning (and here we might return to the opening words of Section I). This is the 'pattern' of a poem or a piece of music: their beginning knows their end, for the end is the cause of the beginning.

> Or say that the end precedes the beginning,
> And the end and the beginning were always there
> Before the beginning and after the end.
> And all is always now.

What is suggested is the 'co-existence' of past, present and future so that existence is not simply a transitional passage from past to present to future but a lived experience of meaning and purpose, wholeness and harmony in which past, present and future are coterminous.

What poetry does, then, is by shaping and ordering them to give a fullness of meaning to words that they do not normally possess. Usually, they 'strain,/Crack and sometimes break . . . will not stay in place,/Will not stay still.' Words are assailed by other words, as 'The Word in the desert' (the Logos, or God) was 'attacked by voices of temptation'. Within the pattern of words, or musical notes, or life itself, there is movement, but the movement is given purpose by the pattern.

What, then, is the 'pattern' which gives time its purpose? Eliot's answer comes in one word: 'Love'. This is not the same as 'Desire', for desire suggests attraction and repulsion, movement away and towards. 'Love' is a kind of stillness, a cause and a conclusion, beginning and end. And by 'Love', Eliot means a love of God. Writing about Dante's *Vita Nuova*, Eliot suggested that the modern mind should accustom itself 'to find meaning in *final causes* rather than in origins'. He went on:

> The final cause is the attraction towards God. A great deal of sentiment has been spilt, especially in the eighteenth and nine-teenth centuries, upon idealizing the reciprocal feelings of man and woman towards each other . . . this sentiment ignoring the fact that the love of man and woman (or for that matter of man and man) is only explained and made reasonable by the higher love, or else is simply the coupling of animals (*Selected Essays*, p.274)

'The final cause' is the purpose to which temporal existence intends. For Eliot, life only makes sense if it is seen as having shape and order; otherwise, it is as Sweeney describes it in Eliot's unfinished drama

'Sweeney Agonistes': 'Birth, and copulation, and death. That's all the facts when you come to brass tacks'. Human love is for Eliot a lower manifestation of divine love and the 'final cause' of human life is to experience 'the attraction towards God'.

As we near the poem's conclusion, we hear again the voices of the children in the rose-garden and the quickening excitement is suddenly broken off with the words 'Ridiculous the waste sad time/ Stretching before and after'. Our moments of illumination, or of Love, exist only as isolated pauses in the onward flow of time. We have to accept the 'Ridiculous', 'waste', 'sad' time of past-present-future, the 'before' and 'after', because this is the 'movement' that constitutes the ultimate pattern, a pattern that itself remains for the most part beyond our knowledge but might occasionally be glimpsed.

4 TECHNICAL FEATURES

4.1 SYMBOLISM AND IMAGERY

When Eliot arrived in England from Europe in 1914, to study Greek philosophy at Oxford, he brought with him a profound admiration for some of the nineteenth-century French poets he had read as a student in Paris during 1910–11. The works of Charles Baudelaire, Tristan Corbière and Jules Laforgue, amongst others, exercised a powerful influence on the young Eliot, who was irresistibly drawn towards poetic effects in some French poetry of which most English writers at the turn of the century seemed blithely ignorant. In Baudelaire, Eliot found a poet whose verses, particularly in *Les Fleurs du Mal* (1857), expressed the more sordid aspects of life in the modern metropolis. From Corbière and Laforgue, Eliot adopted a particular tone of mocking irony and grim despair filtered through abrupt changes of tone and imagery. What he found was a poetry which truly registered the modern consciousness: fragmented, unstable and profoundly sceptical. By contrast, what Eliot found in England was, for the most part, a poetry of emotional looseness, of nostalgia and escapism still striving for a vanished world of pastoral contentment. In bringing into English certain French techniques, Eliot was striving to restore to English poetry the sinewy muscularity, the emotional exactness and intellectual intensity of some of the seventeenth-century English poets and dramatists he most admired. To recover a vital tradition in English poetry Eliot had to effect a revolution.

One aspect of that 'revolution' involved taking over from French poetry a procedure we identify, all too loosely, as 'Symbolism'. This is a term unfortunately so various in its application that we cannot now hope to define it very precisely. But let us begin by taking a simple example. We may say that the Union Jack is a symbol of the United Kingdom: we have here a relationship between a particular configuration of shapes and colours (the flag) and the abstract idea (the country) for which it stands. Thus, the symbol is an object which 'stands for', or expresses, something other than itself, and in the case of the flag we are taught by agreed convention that the signifier – the flag – stands in a clear relation to the signified – the country. Symbols, then, can have a clearly identifiable significance in this way when we recognise a direct relationship between the object and the thing for which it stands.

Sometimes the relationship is not so direct: water may 'stand for' not only life-giving properties but also for death (by drowning) and Eliot is very conscious of such ambiguities in his use of such symbols. But the relationship between signifier and signified may be rather more strained. Suppose that what I want to express is not a particular 'thing' or body of ideas but a particular state of mind or a complex of emotions. In this sort of case, we are inevitably drawn towards a more private or subjective symbolism whereby the relationship between signifier and signified is much more tenuous and less direct. For all of us, at one time or another, a particular feeling or experience seems to be encapsulated by something which appears far removed from it: a particular sense-impression of colour, taste, sound or smell may suddenly prompt a surge of emotion. And this is often the way in which the Symbolist poetry read by Eliot works: we are given a signifier from which the signified has receded a good deal.

Hence Symbolism is inevitably suggestive. Ideas and emotions are not directly described or overtly defined, but suggested by evocative symbols. Such poetry may have a haunting indefiniteness (one recalls Eliot's notorious phrase about poetry communicating before it is understood) – or a quite impenetrable obscurity. In the end, we may well want to decide that some symbols are best left unexplained, that we must allow them to exert their powerful suggestiveness rather than pursue a fugitive equation between the 'symbol' and what it 'stands for'. Take, for example, the case of Eliot's three white leopards in *Ash-Wednesday*. There they sit under a juniper-tree, an unblemished white, reposeful and self-satisfied after having consumed the organs and flesh of a human body. What are we to make of them? What do they 'stand for'? Source-hunting does not really help us. Let them remain in the imagination: powerful and docile; cruel and benign; beautiful and terrifying.

All this is not to say that Eliot was a 'Symbolist' poet but rather to suggest that much of the power and 'meaning' of his poetry resides in his use of symbols (such as water, fire, and other symbols drawn from Dante or the Bible) and images. Briefly, we may say that images are comparisons which are explicit (a simile) or implicit (a metaphor). Why is an evening like a patient etherised on a table? Why is the corner of a woman's eye like a crooked pin? Why is the activity of the memory like a madman shaking a dead geranium? Eliot's early poetry often makes these startling images. We might well try to tease out the details of the comparison: like a madman, the memory throws together ('shakes') in an incoherent, dislocated way things which were once beautiful and vital but now withered, like the dead geranium. But to 'explain' these images, you must first 'feel' them – for what Eliot's symbolism and imagery achieve is the unification of thought and feeling, so that intellect and emotion are simultaneously engaged.

What Eliot also found in French Symbolist poetry – as in some seventeenth-century English poets such as John Donne – was the rapid transition from one symbol or image to another with the connection remaining implicit. So, for example, in one stanza of the 'Preludes' we abruptly shift from a cat eating butter to a child pocketing a toy to eyes peering through shutters to a crab gripping a stick, with no connecting thread between them apparent. So we have to collaborate with the poet and it may take some time before a coherence emerges. Indeed, we may have to go one step further and recognise that the effect relies not on the flow of associated images but on the gaps, the interstices, between them. What some of Eliot's poetry presents us with is the difficulty of saying anything at all. What we have is a kind of language-in-the-making, thoughts and feelings that tremble on the edge of expression.

4.2 METRE AND RHYME

One of the ways by which Eliot signalled his revolution was in his use of unfamiliar verse-structures. Indeed, many of Eliot's first readers would have been hard pressed to see any structure at all in his early poems, so shockingly new did they appear. Again, Eliot had learned from his French poets that the rich suggestiveness of Symbolism could not consort with the organised regularity of traditional forms and structures. The French poets were intent on breaking the tyranny of the alexandrine, a metrical unit of twelve syllables such as is to be found in Keat's line about a creature 'which líke a wóunded snáke drags íts slow léngth alóng'. Before too long, French 'vers libérés' – freed verse – became 'vers libres' – free verse, whereby the poem adheres to no regular metre or form. What we find in Eliot's early poetry is a disruption of regularity. If in his use of symbols and images we find an abruptness of transition so that they are juxtaposed with one another, so in Eliot's verse-structures we find the same dislocation and fragmentariness.

Eliot's early poetry – 'The Love Song of J. Alfred Prufrock', 'Portrait of a Lady', 'Preludes', 'Rhapsody on a Windy Night' – does adhere to a metrical organisation. However, the disruption comes about because in any one verse-paragraph (and we feel they are too irregular to be called stanzas) Eliot might juxtapose lines of different metrical length. Take for example, the opening of 'The Love Song'.

Lines of three stresses ('Let us gó then, yóu and Í . . . The múttering retréats . . . of insídióus intént') lie with other lines which can be scanned as a regular iambic pentameter, an arrangement of ten alternating unstressed and stressed syllables as in 'Of réstless nights in óne-night chéap hotéls/And sáwdust réstauránts with óyster-shélls'. The effect of this is one of nervous agitation as the lines refuse to settle into strict regularity – and the nervous agitation, of course, is Prufrock's. So when the metre does settle into regularity it does so with a particular effect. The lines about Hamlet (111–19) are in a strict iambic pentameter which self-consciously recalls the movement of Shakespeare's dramatic verse. Similarly, the lines 'I should have been a pair of ragged claws/Scuttling across the floors of silent seas' achieve an anguished definiteness because of their metrical regularity achieved amidst irregularity.

Visible in the early poetry is a governing principle of metrical arrangement. Sometimes, though, Eliot composes his metres not just according to a metronomic regularity but also according to natural speech patterns to which he gives shape. His lines are so arranged as to catch the rhythms of contemporary speech so that what we hear is not a particular metre but a particular voice. Lines are arranged so that the emphasis might fall naturally into a pattern of speech and vocal inflexion:

> Well! and what if she should die some afternoon,
> Afternoon grey and smoky, evening yellow and rose;
> Should die and leave me sitting pen in hand
> With the smoke coming down above the housetops . . .

This, we feel, is natural speech given shape and order so that the emotions behind it – guilt and relief – are palpably felt in the movement of the words.

The progression of Eliot's poetry shows a movement away from metrical forms towards an exploration of speech-rhythms (and this is hardly surprising in view of Eliot's interest in dramatic verse). In this respect, an obvious comparison offers itself in the *Poems 1920* selection. This contains a number of poems written in quatrains with a strict metre and the contrast between their taut regularity and the looseness of 'Gerontion' could not be more startling. The disorder of 'Gerontion', we may say, represents the disorder in Eliot himself as he gropes towards an understanding of his own spiritual condition. The lines are composed not simply to satisfy a metrical pattern, but also as a way of measuring the weight and pace of the speaking voice. Hence, the line 'To be eaten, to be divided, to be drunk' echoes in its rhythm as in its words the utterance of the priest in the sacrament of communion. The section beginning at line 33 disposes the sentence-structure over the line-endings so that weight is given to certain phrases which have an almost prayer-like sonority: 'Think now . . . Think now . . . Gives too late . . . Gives too soon . . . ' and this structure is echoed in the following section: 'Think at last . . . Think at last . . . '.

But 'Gerontion' does not abandon metre. It is certainly less evident than the alternating light and heavy stresses of the earlier poems we have mentioned; it is now more freely disposed to catch the stresses of speech patterns, and the position of pauses within lines is more varied. There are lines which fall easily into an iambic pattern: 'An óld man ín a dráughty hóuse . . . She gíves when óur attention ís distrácted . . . We háve not réached conclúsion, whén I/stíffen in a rénted hóuse . . . '. But in 'Gerontion' Eliot is attempting, not wholly successfully, to find some other structural principle than that of metrical organisation. It is *The Hollow Men* which marks a new phase in Eliot's experiments with metre. The lines are arranged not according to a pattern of stresses, but of phrasing. The effect is altogether more incantatory, more like a chant or, significantly, more like a prayer. And, of course, it is with a broken prayer that the poem ends.

This prayer-like quality becomes even more prominent in the later religious poems – *Ash-Wednesday*, 'Journey of the Magi' and 'Burnt Norton'. It is achieved by a principle of repetitiousness, of word, of phrasing and of rhythmical units. An obvious example is the litany in Section II of *Ash-Wednesday*, or the modified repetition of the poem's opening lines at the beginning of Section VI. In 'Journey of the Magi' the lines for the most part are composed according to the natural stresses and pauses of a speaking voice, with significant exceptions. The dislocation of 'but set down/This set down/This' catches the sudden urgency of the speaker and a few lines later the run on of 'this Birth was/Hard and bitter agony for us' throws all the emphasis of agonised surprise onto the word 'Hard'. In 'Burnt Norton' Eliot uses a four-stress line ('Tíme présent and tíme pást/Are bóth perhaps présent in tíme fúture') as the norm from which he departs and to which he returns to create varied effects of lyricism – a lyricism which is nevertheless rendered in the inflexions of natural speech.

We can observe the same movement towards incantation in Eliot's use of rhyme. In the early poems, rhyme is irregular and used for local effects: to set up the mock-lyrical opening of 'The Love Song' or the bathos of 'go/Michelangelo'. In 'Preludes', the rhyming is elaborate, binding the lines together and contributing to the musical effects promised in the poem's title. But in *The Hollow Men* rhyme has become part of the poem's structure, integral to the structure of repetitiousness. The opening section obsessively emphasises its rhymes: 'men . . . when'; 'Alas! . . . meaningless . . . grass . . . glass'; 'together . . . cellar'. In lines 19-28, the vision of harmony is

caught in the full rhymes: 'column . . . solemn . . . '; 'swinging . . . singing'; 'are . . . star'. The supple fluidity of *Ash-Wednesday* and 'Burnt Norton' is partly created by the frequent repetition of
vowel sounds not only as rhymes at line-endings but also within lines.
For example, read aloud lines 107–16 of *Ash-Wednesday* and listen to
the way the sound captures a sensuous fullness and immediacy.

4.3 SYNTAX: POETRY AS MUSIC

Amongst the ways in which Eliot explored the resources of language
were his experiments with syntax – the arrangement of words so as to
compose a sentence. It is often the syntax which makes some of his
poems appear puzzling and alarming. His disruption of syntax was
part of his effort of forcing, or even dislocating, language into his
meaning. It also contributes to the musical effects of his poetry.
Indeed, one of the avowed aims of the French Symbolist poets was to
recover from music what they thought properly belonged to poetry.
This could be done in an obvious way by exploiting the simple fact
that words make sounds, and that the sounds of words might
contribute to their sense (a ready example is the literary device of
onomatopoeia which describes a word whose sound, such as 'click',
mimics its sense). But musicality could also be achieved in another
way, by allowing poems the indefiniteness and suggestiveness of
music. We cannot comfortably say of a piece of music that it 'means'
so-and-so: it may suggest all sorts of emotions simultaneously. Music,
too, is based on continuity, on sounds which progress from one
another successively. Indeed, we might say of music that the experience of continuity is all that it can truly present to us, the notes
making constructions which are modified, departed from, returned
to, restated and brought to rest. We might note how many of Eliot's
titles refer us to music: a love song, preludes, a rhapsody, a quartet.
In the syntactical arrangement of words, Eliot sometimes aims for
effects of continuity or suspension which are akin to music.

   This is perhaps more true of the later than the earlier poems. 'The
Love Song', 'Portrait of a Lady', 'Preludes' and 'Rhapsody on a
Windy Night' are punctuated according to the conventional rules of
syntax. Sometimes complication arises in our reading of the poems
simply because the sentences are lengthy. Many of the verse-
paragraphs in 'The Love Song' compose a single sentence and it is the
very length of the sentence, uncoiling through its subordinate clauses,
which carries the effect of boredom and languor. In the 'Preludes'
and 'Rhapsody on a Windy Night' the heavy stresses and lengthy
sentences capture a sense of fatigue, of the dragging weight of time
itself. But in 'Gerontion' we find at the very opening a syntactical

complication which is a very part of the poem's meaning. The speaker tells us that

> I was neither at the hot gates
> Nor fought in the warm rain
> Nor knee deep in the salt marsh, heaving a cutlass,
> Bitten by flies, fought.

Why the repetition of 'fought'? Syntax requires that the word need occur only once, so why does Eliot duplicate it? What the lines describe is action, and the energy of fighting is caught in the agitated rhythm and muscular consonants. But of course what Gerontion says is that he *did not* fight and the negatives only gain prominence when, paradoxically, we reach the last word, 'fought', which because of its place in the syntax is suddenly limp and lame. The word is dead, inert, drained of energy, as exhausted and empty as Gerontion himself. Later in the same poem we find:

> In the juvescence of the year
> Came Christ the tiger

> In depraved May, dogwood and chestnut . . .

Why is there no full stop after 'tiger'? Why the incomplete line and the gap before we continue? It is as if the mention of Christ as tiger, the devourer, stops the poet dead in his tracks. There is an appalled pause, a suspension in the language mirroring the poet's own hesitation before the figure of Christ. In these cases, we find Eliot's use of syntax contributing to the overall poetic meaning.

In *The Hollow Men* we find a challenging absence of conventional punctuation. It is as if the hollow men are struggling to utter anything at all: 'Our dried voices, when/We whisper together/Are ·quiet and meaningless . : . '. 'Their 'lost kingdoms' are a 'broken jaw' and they 'avoid speech'. The poem collapses into unpunctuated fragments – 'For Thine is/Life is/For Thine is the' – as if the 'Shadow' has fractured them. Only at one point in the poem does the language flow more confidently. The speaker thinks of the eyes he dare not meet 'There', where

> voices are
> In the wind's singing
> More distant and more solemn
> Than a fading star.

We would normally expect the verb 'are' to come later in the sentence (after 'singing'). As it stands, the verb, pointed up by the rhyme, is curiously vulnerable and exposed, gratefully saying that 'There' voices and singing 'are'. By his control of syntax, Eliot renders the feeling of wonderment.

The opening of *Ash-Wednesday* looks as if its language is heading for collapse, just as it did in *The Hollow Men*:

> Because I do not hope to turn again
> Because I do not hope
> Because I do not hope to turn . . .

But suddenly the language recovers to compose a thrilling music. These opening lines, unpunctuated and repetitious, enact their own sort of 'turning', hesitating and circling before arriving at the main verb – 'I no longer strive'. The 'music' of *Ash-Wednesday* is achieved by the lightness of punctuation, a repetitiousness resembling a liturgical chant and, quite remarkably, a use of silence. Take the close of Section III where the final line, 'but speak the word only', after a long pause finally 'speaks' in answer to the threatened despair of 'Lord, I am not worthy'. Or take the close of Section IV. After the appeal to 'Redeem the time, redeem the dream . . . Till the wind shake a thousand whispers from the yew' we subside to 'And after this our exile' – with a blank silence following it. We might fill out that silence for ourselves if we know the words of the prayer to the Virgin Mary: 'and after this our exile show unto us the blessed fruit of thy womb, Jesus'. The poem leads us towards this silence, towards a contemplation of what cannot be put into words. The challenge it throws down to conventional syntax and language is that they do not say enough, that they cannot express the divine.

As a final example of Eliot's manipulation of (or escape from) syntax, look at the opening of Section IV in *Ash-Wednesday*. Beginning 'Who walked between the violet and the violet . . . ' we seem at first to have a question. As the interrogative ('who') is repeated, so we await the question mark – which never arrives. And so the 'who' is silently transformed from an interrogative into a statement with the subject ('The woman who' or 'She who') unstated. It is as if to nominate the subject would be to desecrate it: it is present but tantalisingly hidden, an incipient force in the syntax as in Eliot's life.

Eliot's use of syntax, then, is a part of his procedure to force language into attempting to say the unsayable. It is an instrument in his 'raid on the inarticulate'.

4.4 THE USE OF ALLUSION

One of the most obvious difficulties which Eliot's poetry presents to the reader is the learned scholarship it bears. There is no blinking the fact of Eliot's erudition: he was widely read in European literature (including, of course, classical antiquity), in anthropology, psychology, philosophy and theology. His scholarship is everywhere present in his poems, whether it be in the use of French models for his earliest poetry or in the philosophical explorations of the later. But Eliot did not parade his learning for its own sake. His passionate engagement with man's intellectual explorations was for Eliot a matter of personal discovery, of locating himself in a context of historical development, of accounting for his own nature and the nature of twentieth-century life. He wrote in the consciousness not only of using various intellectual traditions, but of adding to them as well. Eliot's allusiveness – the explicit or implicit references he makes to other literature or to established bodies of thought – is another of the strategies by which he attempts to express himself more completely in his poems.

Eliot's allusiveness, then, is a way of incorporating himself and his work in a particular tradition. As I have described elsewhere (see pp.7–9), Eliot conceived of tradition not as something locked into the past but as a living presence existing contemporaneously with him. He refers to other works of literature not as a gesture towards the past but as a way of bringing the past into the present. Hence the purpose of his epigraphs is to announce a parallel situation to the one described in the poem. So, for example, the epigraph to 'The Love Song of J. Alfred Prufrock' speaks of a figure in Hell talking to one who is presumed to remain in Hell and thus to whom the truth might be safely revealed. So the poem itself is declared to be an attempt to tell the truth of the twentieth-century urban Hell in which Prufrock exists. The poem's references to Andrew Marvell, John Donne, Shakespeare and Chaucer (amongst others) are ways of saying that Prufrock's/Eliot's situation is not unique, that the problem of Prufrock is inherent in all men at all times. Marvell, Donne, Shakespeare, Chaucer are still with us because, like Eliot, they addressed the essential, unchanging conditions of man's existence.

It is often said that Eliot's allusions to past writers is his way of measuring the present age against past ages to find the present more dishevelled, squalid and despairing. Certainly it is true that the urgency in his allusiveness springs from his conviction that the modern age, for its survival, needs to recover its roots and return to its civilising sources (one of which, for example, would be Christian belief). Eliot's writings everywhere show a revulsion from contemporary civilisation, its materialism, philistinism and mass uniformity. The opening of 'Sweeney Erect', for example, summons up the world of classical mythology in a language that is reverentially elevated, richly poetic and, ultimately, nostalgic for a world of heroic passion and endeavour. Eliot's allusions are a way of condemning the present, but they do not simply refer us longingly to a lost Golden Age. Eliot is also creating antecedents for himself. He looks back into history not to lament its remoteness but to find recurring patterns of existence: suffering and (possible) salvation. From the beginning, Eliot perceived history not as a linear sequence of events but as patterns of recurrence and his allusions are ways of describing that recurrence. It should come as no surprise, then, that Eliot's later work is drawn more and more to a conception of infinity not as an endless sequence of passing time but as the absence of time, as *stillness*, a continuing 'now'. In his use of allusions to suggest the continuing presence of the past, Eliot is expressing a circular rather than linear view of history. Man's predicament does not essentially change.

Eliot's allusions often come in the form of a modified or disguised quotation and we may take a single example – almost at random – to see the resonance it achieves. In 'The Love Song of J. Alfred Prufrock' the speaker asks

> Would it have been worth while,
> To have bitten off the matter with a smile,
> To have squeezed the universe into a ball
> To roll it toward some overwhelming question,
> To say: 'I am Lazarus, come from the dead . . . '

The image of squeezing something into a ball and rolling it echoes the close of Andrew Marvell's 'To his Coy Mistress', a passionate poem of seduction in which the speaker urges the unwilling girl:

> Let us roll all our strength and all
> Our sweetness up into one ball,
> And tear our pleasures with rough strife
> Thorough the iron gates of life.
> Thus, though we cannot make our sun
> Stand still, yet we will make him run.

Marvell's speaker vehemently (and, of course, speciously – but his seduction is a game of persuasion) asserts that by consummating their passion the couple will win some sort of ascendancy over life. Time will not stand still for them, but by full-blooded passion they will live life to the full and have a mastery over time by not wasting it: they will break through life's constraints (its 'iron gates') into a more fulfilling life. Now, Eliot's Prufrock is obsessed with time: time as occupied by endless routine, habit, tedium, time being wasted. He might make something of his life by having the courage to ask some 'overwhelming question' (the question was never so overwhelming to Marvell's determined seducer!) or to tell some overwhelming truth about life and death (such as the resurrected Lazarus might have told). But Prufrock's mounting determination abruptly withers, for he can only foresee the woman to whom he might address the question receiving it with haughty distaste: ' "That is not what I meant at all./That is not it, at all" '. Eliot refers to Marvell's poem as a way of measuring Prufrock's inadequacy. The stirrings of passion in Prufrock are stifled at birth and he remains the hesitant, tongue-tied, ineffectual anti-type of the Marvellian lover.

Eliot makes his allusions in other ways than by overt or covert quotation. On many occasions it is his style which is imitative. The early poems are at times highly derivative of the style of the French Symbolists, particularly Jules Laforgue and Théophile Gautier. In 'The Love Song', the passage beginning 'No! I am not Prince Hamlet . . . ' has the muscular verve and dash of Elizabethan dramatic verse. In this respect, it is worth noting how many of Eliot's poems are dramatic monologues spoken by created personae: Prufrock, an unnamed associate of the Lady, Gerontion, one of the Magi, and Eliot was much preoccupied by the notion of a truly contemporary dramatic verse. Eliot's stylistic effects as well as his allusions often return us to the great Elizabethan dramatists about whom Eliot wrote: Marlowe, Shakespeare, Jonson, Middleton, Heywood, Tourneur, Webster, Ford, Massinger and Marston.

What Eliot's allusions attempt to achieve, then, is a synthesis of past and present. He introduces into his poetry references to past literature so as to assert a unity with it. It was thus inevitably the case that as Eliot found himself drawn towards Christianity his work should draw on two principal sources of Christian understanding: the poetry of Dante and the Bible. The later poems are so suffused with such references that 'allusion' is an inadequate description. By the time of his conversion, Eliot's poems do not refer to these texts but rather take root in them as assertions of faith.

5 SPECIMEN COMMENTARY

To practise the sort of task you might be asked to undertake in an exam, turn to *Ash-Wednesday*, Section IV, lines 18–32 ('The new years walk . . . And after this our exile'). A typical examination question might be:

(a) Explain and comment on any two allusions contained in the passage.
(b) How does the style of the passage help to convey the meaning and feeling of the poet?

To begin, you should look at the questions closely to make sure you have fully understood them. The first one requires you to identify in the passage the sources of two references to other works. But it also asks you to 'comment' on them, to say why you think Eliot wanted to make such references and what they contribute to the meaning. The second question is broader in scope. The word 'style' should call to mind such things as imagery, use of symbols, rhythm, the sounds of words, and so on. 'How' – in what ways – do these things communicate 'meaning' and 'feeling'? Notice there are *two* requirements here: the examiner will expect an answer to relate poetic style to both the meaning of the passage and to its emotional qualities.
(a) '*Redeem/The time*'   Eliot is recalling a phrase of St Paul's in the Epistles by which he exhorted the early Christians to lead lives of such personal virtue as would set an example to the whole age in which they lived. The reference is one of *Ash-Wednesday*'s many religious allusions. It is an appeal to the figure of the Lady for her divine intercession so that the speaker can be helped in the reformation of his spiritual life. The allusion suggests that the speaker sees himself in an historical situation akin to the early Christians, living in a spiritual dark age which only faith can enlighten. This kind of reaching back in history for parallels and analogies to the poet's

personal situation makes the poem seem more impersonal and universal in scope.

'*And after this our exile*'   These words are taken from a prayer to the Virgin Mary which ends: 'and after this our exile show unto us the blessed fruit of thy womb, Jesus'. The idea of 'exile', of being an outcast, is supported in the imagery of an arid garden ('the dry rock' and 'the sand') which is given life by 'the silent sister' in the springing fountain and the bird-song. But perhaps the most telling significance of the quotation is its incompleteness. It is as if the poet dare not ask, or dare not hope, to be shown 'the fruit of thy womb': Christ himself. The reference, like so much else in the poem, is an expression of hope wrestling with despair. The poet is aware of himself as an 'exile' but is unsure of whether 'the fruit of thy womb' will be revealed to him and restore him to true spiritual life.

(b)   The passage describes a vision of a robed figure who restores fertility to a lifeless garden and who offers the poet the hope of spiritual renewal and blessedness. It conveys a sense of intense excitement, of enthralled awe and exultation.

The opening section of the excerpt expresses itself in visionary terms. The veiled figure embodies 'The new years' of a new life which redeems the waste and follies of the past. There may be regret ('tears') for the past but the tears are transformed into 'a bright cloud' by the presence of the Lady. This image of startling illumination (rather than the gloom we usually associate with 'cloud') suggests how the presence of the Lady has transformed the speaker's past. A triumphant brightness is portrayed again in the vision of 'jewelled unicorns' drawing by a 'gilded hearse'. These symbols are taken from Dante's *Divine Comedy* at the moment when Dante glimpses his beloved Beatrice. If the 'hearse' suggests death, it is in this image a death made glorious. Now, as if in answer to the plea to 'Redeem/ The time', the robed figure of the 'silent sister' bends her head. She is pictured 'Between the yews' (trees associated with death) and 'behind the garden god' (a statue of Priapus or Pan, representing the pre-Christian, pagan world). His flute is 'breathless', as if the sculpture is incapable of being brought to life or giving life. The nun-like figure (whose garments of white and blue are the traditional colours of the Virgin Mary) simply and silently 'signed'. At her signal, water springs from the fountain, a bird sings and life seems to have returned to the garden. Once again, the poet appeals to her to redeem 'The token of the word unheard, unspoken' – a reference to the world's rejection of Christ – until a final triumph is achieved and the unspoken, unheard word finds expression in the 'thousand whispers' shaken by the wind from the yew-tree, symbol now not of death but of life. The excerpt ends with a snatch of prayer which is abruptly halted, not because the mood of exultation suddenly fades but because what remains is perhaps inexpressible.

The meaning of the passage is conveyed in its use of symbols (such as the mysterious Lady, the yew-tree), imagery (for example, the 'bright cloud of tears') and allusions to other religious works (St Paul, St John's Gospel, Dante, a Roman Catholic prayer). But there are other stylistic features which contribute to the expressiveness of the passage. In the first section, the central lines end in verbs ('restoring' and 'Redeem') which give them a pleading urgency. However, the urgency is modified by a confidence felt in the harmony of simple rhymes between 'years' and 'tears', 'rhyme' and 'time', 'Redeem' and 'dream'. As the 'silent sister' makes her signal, so the rhythm grows more regular and confident and at the crucial moment we feel the dramatic hammering of monosyllables: 'bent her head and signed but/spoke no word'. There is suddenly a dramatic pause before the flowing line about fountain and bird-song. Finally, the passage seems to end serenely: the repeated 'w' of the penultimate line makes it quietly liquid. The numerous verbal repetitions in the passage and the absence of punctuation at its conclusion give it a haunting indefiniteness, a quality of dream-like mystery and beauty.

6 CRITICAL DEBATE

It is a critical commonplace to observe that Eliot created the taste by which he is now enjoyed. Inevitably, in his essays and lectures Eliot is to be found making critical judgements about literature which are naturally bound up with his own practice of poetry. In addressing himself to other writers and literary works, Eliot naturally brought into being a climate of opinion which could respond sympathetically to his own poetry. Eliot did not set out to become a central figure in English culture: that he did so testifies to the persuasiveness of his critical insights. In 1956 he delivered a lecture in America attended by an audience of over 13 000: that is the measure of the importance that came to be attached to him not only by his own generation but by younger readers.

Eliot began to attract serious notice after the First World War, when a number of voices were calling for a radical departure from the wistful orthodoxies of the Georgians. At the same time, the growing academic study of English meant that Eliot's critical pronouncements were soon taken up in the new intellectual current. His was a major influence in the restoration of admiration for the Metaphysical poets and Jacobean dramatists; in turn, his own poetry was soon taken up by critics such as F. R. Leavis to show the recovery of a poetic tradition all but lost in the Victorian age. Eliot's critical pronouncements – on tradition, on impersonality, on Metaphysical 'wit' – quickly became the orthodoxies of critical thinking. As for his poetry, even as early as the 1920s the literary editors were complaining of the Eliotic imitators whose Prufrockian verses arrived on their desks all too frequently. *The Waste Land* became a *cri de coeur* for the sensibility of a generation: one might recall Anthony Blanche in Evelyn Waugh's *Brideshead Revisited* declaiming from a college window in Cambridge the lines about 'the young man carbuncular' to an uncomprehending group of sporting hearties.

Yet although Eliot brought into being his own audience, he has left no successors – except to say that nobody interested in twentieth-century poetry and its development can evade the gigantic presence of Eliot. The poets of the 1930s – Auden, Spender, MacNeice, Day Lewis – wrote in a colloquial style given to them by Eliot but were concerned to express themes, attitudes and opinions in a much more direct and easily comprehensible form. In the 1940s came the neo-romantic fervours of, for example, Dylan Thomas – a turning loose of emotion rather than an Eliotic escape from it. The 'Movement' poetry of the 1950s valued an expository rationality far removed from the densities and obliquities of Eliot and by the 1960s his reputation was in decline. Exerting such a seminal influence, Eliot was bound to provoke some sort of counter-revolution. As his poetry became more overtly Christian, many readers felt that there was a weakening in imaginative force and suggested that his earlier work remained his best. Eliot's adherence to a position of 'classicist in literature, royalist in politics, and anglo-catholic in religion' also found disfavour: it smacked too much of highbrow élitism in an age which tried to find a mass popularity for poetry. Sir John Betjeman expressed a widespread opinion when he blamed Eliot for making poetry too difficult for the reader; Philip Larkin was equally sceptical about the bewildering complexities of his poetry. The American critic Yvor Winters was more judicious but just as critical in his view that in expressing the chaos of life Eliot's poetry itself fell into an imitative chaos.

As an Anglo-American, Eliot occupied a curiously ambiguous position on both sides of the Atlantic. He very quickly assimilated himself in English culture and habits with his punctiliously observed manners and formality of speech. Nevertheless, to his first English audience his poetry looked highly exotic and he was almost indissolubly associated with everything that was avant-garde in the artistic movements of the 1920s. To some Americans, however, Eliot came to appear more and more European, more and more conservative and dislocated from the 'genuine' American tradition of Walt Whitman, Ezra Pound, William Carlos Williams, Charles Olson and Allen Ginsberg. In England too it came to be felt that Eliot had distorted a 'true' tradition of native English poetry. Eliot brought back into currency the passionate intellectuality of Metaphysical poets such as John Donne and Andrew Marvell, their challenging rapidity of thought, their daring use of imagery, their dramatic presentation of the speaking voice. But at the same time, his critics assert, he bypassed an authentically English sensibility which is to be found in, say, Thomas Hardy or John Betjeman or Philip Larkin.

There could be no successor to Eliot. As a critic, he introduced an intellectual strictness at just the point when the study of English literature was becoming an independent academic discipline. An illustration comes when he considers Swinburne as a critic: 'Swinburne is an appreciator and not a critic . . . Swinburne stops thinking just at the moment when we are most zealous to go on' (*The Sacred Wood*, Methuen, 1960, pp.19–20). In his first critical excursions Eliot sought an exactness of thinking that is almost scientific: 'The end of the enjoyment of poetry is a pure contemplation from which all the accidents of personal emotion are removed; thus we aim to see the object as it really is . . . ' (*The Sacred Wood*, pp.14–15). His emphasis on the critical vocabulary of 'judgement', 'dissection', and 'analysis' contributed much to what were to become the orthodoxies of literary studies. As a poet he found new resources in the English language for the expression of profound thinking and profound feeling. There is no 'school of Eliot' because only Eliot could do what he did. Although his achievement prompts controversy, his importance stands far above the vagaries of fashion. In his lonely and passionate vocation to the terrors and struggles of poetic creation he has come to stand for succeeding generations of poets as an inimitable exemplar.

REVISION QUESTIONS

1. 'He had to be revolutionary, but only in order to effect a restoration.' What appear to you to be the most revolutionary and conservative tendencies in Eliot's poetry?

2. Write about three of Eliot's poems to show in them a range of personal feeling.

3. How does Eliot achieve vivid images in his poems, and to what symbolic effects does he put them?

4. What does Eliot achieve by his use of personae in his poems?

5. 'It is not poetry, but prose run mad.' To what extent do you find this true of Eliot's poems?

6. Examine the use of allusion in Eliot's poetry.

7. 'A sense of the timeless as well as the temporal': illustrate this comment in the light of Eliot's religious poems.

8. To what extent would you agree that Eliot's poems show a steady progression from despair to religious faith?

9. Examine Eliot's treatment of the theme of love in his poems.

10. 'Genuine poetry can communicate before it is understood.' Have you found this true of any of Eliot's poetry?

FURTHER READING

Ackroyd, P., *T. S. Eliot* (Sphere Books, 1985).

Bergonzi, B., *T. S. Eliot* (Macmillan, 1972).

Edwards, M., *Eliot/Language* (Aquila, 1975).

Eliot, T. S., *Selected Essays* (Faber & Faber, 1951).

Gardner, H., *The Art of T. S. Eliot* (Faber & Faber, 1949).

Kenner, H., *The Invisible Poet: T. S. Eliot* (W. H. Allen, 1960).

Leavis, F. R., *New Bearings in English Poetry* (Chatto & Windus, 1950).

Matthiessen, F. O., *The Achievement of T. S. Eliot* (Oxford University Press, 1958).

Maxwell, D. E. S., *The Poetry of T. S. Eliot* (Routledge & Kegan Paul, 1952).

Southam, B. C., *A Student's Guide to the Selected Poems of T. S. Eliot* (Faber & Faber, 1977).

Spender, S., *Eliot* (Fontana, 1975).

Stead, C. K., *The New Poetic* (Penguin, 1964).

Traversi, D., *T. S. Eliot: The Longer Poems* (Bodley Head, 1976).

Williamson, G., *A Reader's Guide to T. S. Eliot* (Thames & Hudson, 1967).

Wilson, E., *Axel's Castle* (Fontana, 1961).

Mastering English Literature
Richard Gill

Mastering English Literature will help readers both to enjoy
English Literature and to be successful in 'O' levels, 'A' levels
and other public exams. It is an introduction to the study of
poetry, novels and drama which helps the reader in four ways –
by providing ways of approaching literature, by giving examples
and practice exercises, by offering hints on how to write about
literature, and by the author's own evident enthusiasm for the
subject. With extracts from more than 200 texts, this is an
enjoyable account of how to get the maximum satisfaction out
of reading, whether it be for formal examinations or simply
for pleasure.

Work Out English Literature ('A' level)
S.H. Burton

This book familiarises 'A' level English Literature candidates
with every kind of test which they are likely to encounter.
Suggested answers are worked out step by step and accompanied by full author's commentary. The book helps students
to clarify their aims and establish techniques and standards so
that they can make appropriate responses to similar questions
when the examination pressures are on. It opens up fresh ways
of looking at the full range of set texts, authors and critical
judgements and motivates students to know more of these
matters.

MACMILLAN SHAKESPEARE VIDEO WORKSHOPS

DAVID WHITWORTH

Three unique book and video packages, each examining a particular aspect of Shakespeare's work; tragedy, comedy and the Roman plays. Designed for all students of Shakespeare, each package assumes no previous knowledge of the plays and can serve as a useful introduction to Shakespeare for 'O' and 'A' level candidates as well as for students at colleges and institutes of further, higher and adult education.

The material is based on the New Shakespeare Company Workshops at the Roundhouse, adapted and extended for television. By combining the resources of television and a small theatre company, this exploration of Shakespeare's plays offers insights into varied interpretations, presentation, styles of acting as well as useful background information.

While being no substitute for seeing the whole plays in performance, it is envisaged that these video cassettes will impart something of the original excitement of the theatrical experience, and serve as a welcome complement to textual analysis leading to an enriched and broader view of the plays.

Each package consists of:

* the Macmillan Shakespeare editions of the plays concerned;

* a video cassette available in VHS or Beta;

* a leaflet of teacher's notes.

THE TORTURED MIND
looks at the four tragedies Hamlet, Othello, Macbeth and King Lear.

THE COMIC SPIRIT
examines the comedies Much Ado About Nothing, Twelfth Night, A Midsummer Night's Dream, and As You Like It.

THE ROMAN PLAYS
Features Julius Caesar, Antony and Cleopatra and Coriolanus